TIMETABLE PLANNING

Heinemann Organization in Schools Series

General Editor: Michael Marland

Timetable Planning

JOHN BROOKES

HEINEMANN EDUCATIONAL BOOKS
LONDON
in association with
ROYAL INSTITUTE OF
PUBLIC ADMINISTRATION

Heinemann Educational Books
22 Bedford Square, London WC1B 3HH
LONDON   EDINBURGH   MELBOURNE   AUCKLAND   HONG KONG
SINGAPORE   KUALA LUMPUR   IBADAN   NAIROBI   JOHANNESBURG
EXETER (NH)   NEW DELHI   KINGSTON   PORT OF SPAIN

© Royal Institute of Public Administration 1980

First published 1980
Reprinted 1981

British Library C.I.P. Data

Brookes, John
   Timetable planning — (Organization in schools series)
   1. Schedules, School
   I. Title II. Series
   371. 2′42   LB1038
   ISBN 0-435-80150-3

Photoset and printed in Malta by
Interprint Limited

Contents

Acknowledgement and Dedication

Inevitably many more people were involved in this book than can be mentioned here, most of them unknowingly. I would however like to thank all the timetablers whose problems I have had the misfortune to be involved with.

Particular thanks are due to my one-time colleagues Colin Dixon and Mike Zarraga for their initial work on timetable planning.

If any one person inspired this book it is Dr Harald Michalsen. His work on the mathematics of timetabling and the Nor-Data computer-assisted school timetabling system which he created provided the main source of ideas, concepts and experience for the book. I would therefore like to record here my sincerest thanks, and as some token of my gratitude, to dedicate this book to Dr Michalsen.

J. E. B.

Foreword

The Heinemann Organization in Schools Series is a systematic attempt to help schools improve the quality of the secondary-school experience by a methodical study of aspects of the ways in which schools can be organized. The series has been planned as a whole, so that the central philosophy and every aspect of the planning and running of schools is methodically covered. However, each book has been written by a different author and from a different point of view out of his or her own observation, experience, and conviction. Since each book is written to stand on its own, there is inevitably some overlapping between the volumes, as certain topics (such as pupil choice, or the responsibilities of senior staff) need to be included in a number of books, though with varying degrees of detail and from different points of view.

Clearly the whole process of timetabling is of immense importance in helping a school fulfil its aims. The series therefore devotes two books to aspects of the timetable itself; this one by John Brookes concentrates in great detail and with great analytic power on the stage of timetable *planning*. It is thus complementary to the more general book Neil Ransom is writing for this series. Called *The Comprehensive Timetable,* it will consider the whole process from curriculum planning to implementing the completed timetable.

In the present book, which arises from research undertaken for the Royal Institute of Public Administration, John Brookes has done us all a great service in focusing on the planning stage of timetabling. It is at this point in the process that earlier good schemes can founder because of loose planning; it is also at this stage that later problems can be built up by lack of thoroughness. In his book, Mr Brookes takes us clearly and painstakingly through the stages of planning in a way which will apply to virtually any complex school and which shows the simplicity of the crucial points.

Although this is a book which every timetabler and would-be timetabler will wish to study, for it is really the first account in print of this part of a school's work, it is also written for others in the school, especially heads of department, whose tasks are more effectively carried out if they understand the requirements of timetable planning.

MICHAEL MARLAND

1 Introduction

Few people would seriously debate the crucial role of a timetable in the administration and efficient organization of schools at secondary level and in education establishments at higher levels. Yet strange to say the problems of timetabling have not been the subject of much serious study. It is only recently that any effort at all has been devoted to attempts to introduce a more logical and coherent approach to the subject and little by way of advice and guidance exists either in the literature or in the form of training courses. Most timetablers have thus been obliged to 'learn the trade' from their colleagues and from their own experiences. Strange too that amid the lively and ubiquitous debates on curriculum reform, teaching methods, etc., the voice of the timetabler is rarely to be heard and is seldom encouraged to make its presence felt. Neither do timetablers talk a great deal amongst themselves, with the result that each tends to view his timetable both as more complex and as having more unique qualities than other timetables.

Certainly it is true that, at a somewhat superficial level, time-tables look different from each other. It is also true that the building blocks of each timetable — staff, rooms, classes, curriculum, and time units — are different for each school. But at a more basic level many of these differences disappear. Experience with some hundreds of schools has reinforced the view that there are more similarities than differences, and that many of the differences are, from a timetabling point of view, unimportant.

This brings me to a major point in defining the scope of the book: I am concerned here almost exclusively with timetabling, or to be more exact, with timetable planning. This does not mean that Education is of no interest to me or to timetablers. On the contrary, like most other people involved in education — and many that are not — I tend to have strong views on the subject. My concern here, though, is not to add to the Great Debate on Education and its Philosophy, but to help the timetabler make a better job of realizing the educational goals established for him and to encourage him to take a more active role in their evaluation. The timetable after all is, or should be, the expression in concrete terms of a school's educational philosophy.

'Timetabling' to most people conjures up the image of a harassed headmaster, or more commonly nowadays his deputy, sweating away into the small hours, well plied with black coffee or other stimulants, working perhaps for many weeks, getting through many pencils and rubbers, puzzling with coloured pins, bits of cardboard, Lego sets, and even more sophisticated devices. This is, of course, a part of timetabling. It is not however the central, or even a major concern of this book. The cold-towel-and-black-coffee part of timetabling I call 'timetable construction' and is only one part of the timetabling process. Timetabling is, or should be, a three-stage process.

First comes the thinking stage which can start with the new academic year, and perhaps even earlier than this. The thinking stage is concerned with the formulation of objectives and the bringing together of many influences both internal to the school and external to it. 'Is the present timetable meeting all the demands made on it?' 'Are there new ideas in education that we want to try out in the next timetable?' 'What sort of option scheme are we going to introduce in next year's fourth year?' 'Are we doing enough in the remedial department?' 'Was the introduction of a second foreign language in the first year a good idea?' These are some of the questions that may need to be considered at the thinking stage and, hopefully, to which general answers will be found. In other words, what are the educational objectives that the next timetable must try to satisfy?

Second comes the planning stage. We know in general terms by the time this stage is reached what it is we want to achieve. The next question is 'can it be done?' Timetable planning is concerned with questions of feasibility; with evaluating in terms of resources and their availability whether or not the educational objectives of a school are workable.

Third comes timetable construction, followed by the clerical task — not to be underestimated — of preparing the timetable for general circulation.

This book is concerned almost solely with the second stage, with timetable planning, although towards the end timetable construction is considered. It is my view that timetable planning has been shamefully neglected; and my hope that this book will do something to help redress the balance. But first to be more specific about what we mean by timetable planning and so define still further the scope of this book.

It is possible to define two types of planning. First there is descriptive planning, concerned mainly with creating a language to describe curriculum structure. This type of planning is treated at length by T. I. Davies[1] and by the Department of Education and Science in their Cosmos courses. The application of curriculum notation and the calculation of 'bonuses' and so on, is undoubtedly of value at a certain level of analysis because it focuses attention on the distribution of resources to the various parts of the curriculum. It is of little value however when it comes to more detailed considerations of the implementation of a curriculum. The second type of planning — diagnostic planning — is complementary to the descriptive kind in that it provides a necessary bridge between general questions of resource allocation and the nuts and bolts of timetable construction. It is this second type of planning with which I am primarily concerned.

The timetabling process

The view of timetabling taken here is very much wider than that of simply putting the timetable together: this much should already be clear. It is also important to emphasize one or two features of the timetabling process. First, timetabling is a dynamic process rather than a static one. That is to say the timetabler is not concerned with finding a solution to a problem with fixed parameters, but is rather concerned with the way these parameters can, and often must be changed as a result of interaction with each other and as a result of other pressures. Second, and stemming from the dynamic nature of the problem, timetabling is an interactive process involving a continual cycle of consultation and modification. In most schools it is common to find that the timetabler needs frequently to consult his heads of department and other members of staff as the process continues.

The timetabler is thus in a very special position in most schools; he is not, or should not be, simply a mechanic who 'puts things together', but rather the focus and arbiter of many — and often conflicting — requirements. His task is to evaluate in practical terms the feasibility of the demands made on the resources available to the school and, by consultation and repeated evaluation, to implement a feasible curriculum by means of the completed timetable. This is not to say of course that the timetabler must be in a position to make educational decisions, although this is an advantage. Nor of course is it to be assumed that there should only be one person involved in timetabling. The point to stress is that consultation plays a central part in the evaluation and construction stages.

By defining discrete stages in the timetabling process it might be supposed that the transition from one stage to another is distinct

[1] T. I. Davies. *School Organization*. Pergamon Press, 1969.

both in terms of content and of chronology; this is seldom the case since the various stages overlap in time, and blend with each other in content.

The timetabling problem

The mathematics of the timetabling problem has attracted — and continues to attract — a great deal of attention. One avenue of research has been concerned with discovering a set of mathematical conditions which is both necessary and sufficient for a solution to realistic timetabling problems. Such a set of conditions could provide a method of proving that, from a given set of requirements, a timetable could be guaranteed. Sadly, no one has yet discovered a set of conditions that is both necessary *and* sufficient for the solution to most practical timetabling problems. There are however a great many necessary conditions. Although it is not my intention to discuss mathematics, a simple example will help to clarify this fundamental difficulty with timetabling problems. Suppose that in a given school there are forty periods in the week and that a particular teacher is required to teach forty-one periods. Quite obviously it is impossible to produce a timetable that meets this requirement. However, even if the teacher in question is persuaded to teach only forty periods (and this should not be too difficult!), there is still no guarantee that a timetable can be produced that satisfies all other requirements. To ask a teacher to teach 41/40 periods violates a *necessary* condition, but even though the requirement is adjusted so that the necessary condition is satisfied, there is still no guarantee that a timetable exists. The best that can be done is to satisfy as many necessary conditions as one can think of, since this increases one's chances of producing a timetable without too many *ad hoc* compromises.

One of the main objectives of concentrating effort at the time-table planning stage is to eliminate the more obvious violations of necessary conditions. This is not solely to make timetable construction an easier task, although this is undoubtedly a welcome result. In addition there is the considerable advantage that necessary changes in timetable requirements can be made with a cooler head at the earlier planning stage than at the often frantic construction stage when there is usually considerable pressure. It is also true that compromises made at the construction stage can be more drastic and damaging in terms of timetable 'quality' than considered modifications made as the necessary result of careful planning. This too adds weight to the argument for more time and effort to be devoted to planning.

The object of this book therefore is to provide the timetabler with basic techniques that can help him in his timetable planning, and it may be reassuring at this early stage to say that the emphasis is on practical applications rather than on abstruse mathematical devices. Doubtless the mathematics underlying the methods suggested would prove of interest to some, but I have decided that a more down-to-earth and easily assimilable approach is likely to be of greater value to the majority of readers. Doubtless too the techniques offered do not form a complete answer to the problems of planning and construction, but at least a start has been made in what I hope is the right direction!

A word of warning though! It should be made clear right at the start that in practice there will often be a conflict between what is desirable from the timetabler's point of view and what is desirable from an educational point of view. This book is written almost entirely from the timetabler's viewpoint and is intended to help him survive the heat of the summer without too much of a strain. I have deliberately avoided discussion of what is 'good' educationally; first, because this is best left to those whose proper business is education, and second, because it is unnecessary and out of place in considering planning techniques. Having said this I must of course insist that educational considerations should play a dominant role in shaping the timetable; I simply wish to set this dominance in perspective.

A word too about the structure of the book. In Chapter 2 I introduce some basic concepts that crop up throughout the book. Chapter 3 is concerned with resource planning, and in Chapters 4–8 I describe some general methods of analysis that can be used in assessing timetable feasibility. Rather than claim that there is a technique to suit every circumstance — this would be presumptuous — I have tried to cover in broad terms at least some of the more commonly encountered problems. Unless the sample of some hundreds of timetables with which I have had experience has been totally unrepresentative, then I should have covered a good deal of useful ground. But there is usually a gap between general ideas and techniques and the specifics of a given case, so in Chapter 9 I have tried to close this gap somewhat by presenting a case study chosen to illustrate how planning can be used in a real case. It is important to realize that the methods described are only a starting point and that these methods will almost inevitably need to be modified and adapted to suit the particular problems to be solved. There is nothing like experience, so Chapter 10 is designed as a teach-yourself exercise in planning, which even if not a thorough course, should at least be fun!

2 Basic concepts

At the risk of being tedious at the outset, I must start with a few definitions. Although I have tried to keep jargon and technical terms to the very minimum, this cannot always be avoided. Where technical terms are used, these are explained on the spot, but the following definitions will, I hope, be a suitable initial preparation.

RESOURCE — the term 'resource' is used throughout this book to include teachers, classes, rooms and time. To be complete, but not always very useful, one might add 'academic content' as a fifth resource.

ACTIVITY — an activity is a requirement for a given set of resources. 'Class 3B for five periods of English with Mr Blake, in a classroom', is an activity and so too is, 'All the fifth-year classes with fourteen teachers for five periods of option C'. 'Activity' and 'subject' are not necessarily synonymous.

CONFLICT — activities with common resources are said to be in conflict. Conflicting requirements cannot be timetabled simultaneously.

CURRICULUM CYCLE — a general term to mean the period of time before the timetable repeats itself.

I have also used the convention of referring to teacher resources by numbers rather than by initials or names on the grounds that numbers are easier to work with. S, D, T, and Q mean single, double, triple, and quadruple respectively.

3 Resource planning

One of the major causes of difficulty with timetable construction is an apparent lack of appreciation, by heads of department and timetablers alike, of the simple fact that there are, from a timetabling point of view, desirable and undesirable ways of combining resources. Most, if not all, secondary schools have curricula of a sort that require resources to be combined in various ways. The introduction of setting arrangements, for example, requires that a group of classes are brought together with a team of teachers for a part of the curriculum cycle. Subjects like craft, science, and physical education frequently make similar demands for the simultaneous availability of many resources. Option schemes, by definition, also require teams of teachers and combinations of other resources. In many schools this type of requirement is so prevalent as to dominate the curriculum at nearly every level and it is thus of central importance to consider the advantages and disadvantages of alternative ways of combining resources.

A very simple example will serve to illustrate the crucial effect on timetable feasibility of combining resources: three teachers 01, 02, and 03, are each required to teach thirty periods in a forty-period week. Provided that each teacher is treated independently then there is clearly no difficulty — thirty 'goes into' forty with room to spare. Suppose though that these three teachers are required to teach in pairs as follows:

01 and 02 together for 15 periods
02 and 03 together for 15 periods
01 and 03 together for 15 periods

While we have not altered the workload of any teacher, we have produced an impossible timetabling situation by combining them.

It is not however the fact that we have combined teachers that *of itself* makes for this kind of situation. It is the particular way of combining them that is important (Figure 3.1).

Alternative methods of combining resources are best illustrated by a simple example. Suppose that the mathematics department of a school consists of six members of staff (01, 02, 03, 04, 05, 06) and

Fig. 3.1   The three teacher problem

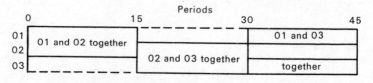

that the curriculum requires mathematics to be set by half-year groups throughout the five years of the school. Each half-year group consists of three classes, and three teachers are required for each half-year group. Each half-year group has five periods of mathematics. Since there are $5 \times 2 = 10$ half-year groups in the school each requiring five periods of mathematics we have a requirement for $10 \times 5 = 50$ periods of mathematics. And since each period requires three teachers there are $50 \times 3 = 150$ teaching periods to be covered by the six staff. Assume further that each teacher is to teach twenty-five periods in a thirty-five-period week. Figure 3.2 shows one of many possible ways of allocating the six staff to satisfy the requirements of the curriculum.

In Figure 3.2 we see, for example, that teachers 01, 02 and 03 are combined as a team for half-year group 1, teachers 01, 04 and 05 provide the team for half-year group 2, and so on. Examination of the teams reveals that every team has at least one member of staff in common with every other team. For example, the team for half-year group 1 (01, 02, 03) has teacher 01 in common with half-year groups 2, 3, 4, and 5, teacher 02 in common with half-year groups 4, 6, 7, and 8, and teacher 03 in common with half-year groups 3, 7, 9, and 10. Teams with a common member are in conflict and therefore cannot be timetabled simultaneously. In this case this means that each of the ten half-year groups requires a *unique* set of five periods and that therefore $10 \times 5 = 50$ unique periods are required to timetable the mathematics department. With only thirty-five periods to play with this is clearly impossible, as is shown in Figure 3.3.

Fig. 3.2   Allocation of overlapping teams

Half-year groups

	1	2	3	4	5	6	7	8	9	10
01	X	X	X	X	X					
02	X			X		X	X	X		
03	X		X				X		X	X
04		X		X		X			X	X
05		X			X		X	X	X	
06			X		X	X		X		X

Teachers

Fig. 3.3   Consequences of overlapping teams

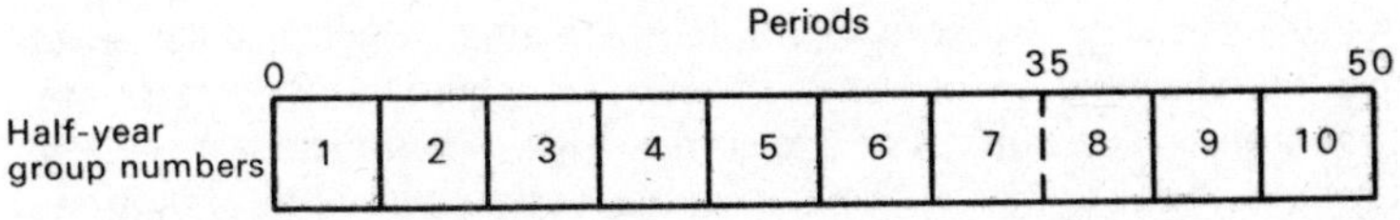

Periods

The example discussed was, of course, an extreme one, although by no means as uncommon as its extremity might suggest. Look now at another extreme shown in Figure 3.4. Here we see that, instead of higgledy-piggledy teams, we now have two teams only; teachers 01, 02, 03 allocated to half-year groups 1, 2, 3, 4, and 5, and teachers 04, 05, 06 allocated to groups 6, 7, 8, 9, and 10. These two basic teams have no members of staff in common and are called 'disjoint' or non-overlapping; we are able therefore (if need be) to timetable

Fig. 3.4   Disjoint teams

any half-year group using one team simultaneously with any half-year group using the other team. Figure 3.5 shows only one of the many ways of timetabling these teams in the minimum of twenty-five periods. Two important advantages stand out from Figure 3.5. First, that the mathematics department, solely by rearranging its teams, can now be fitted into a minimum of twenty-five periods as compared with fifty periods initially. In other words the systematic construction of teams makes all the difference between an impossible and a feasible timetabling problem. And second, that in the case where disjoint teams were used there is considerable freedom and flexibility for combining, where necessary, the various half-year groups.

Fig. 3.5   Timetabling of disjoint teams

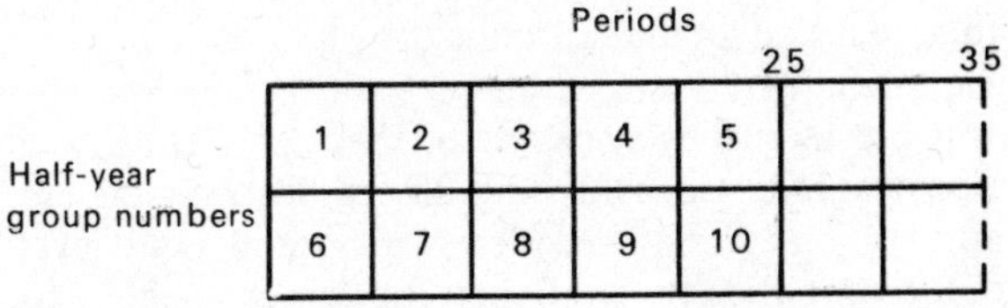

Periods

The Principle of Compatibility

As shown in the previous example, the way in which teacher teams are constructed is of fundamental importance in determining timetabling feasibility. The time is now ripe to define in more general terms a guiding principle for constructing teams of resources, whether these are teachers, classes, rooms, or other resources. This principle is called the 'Principle of Compatibility', and states that, given a universal set of resources a hierarchy of subsets should be chosen such that at any level in the hierarchy these subsets are themselves subsets (proper or otherwise) of the subsets at the next highest level. This is illustrated in Figure 3.6.

Fig. 3.6 Choosing teams with the Principle of Compatibility

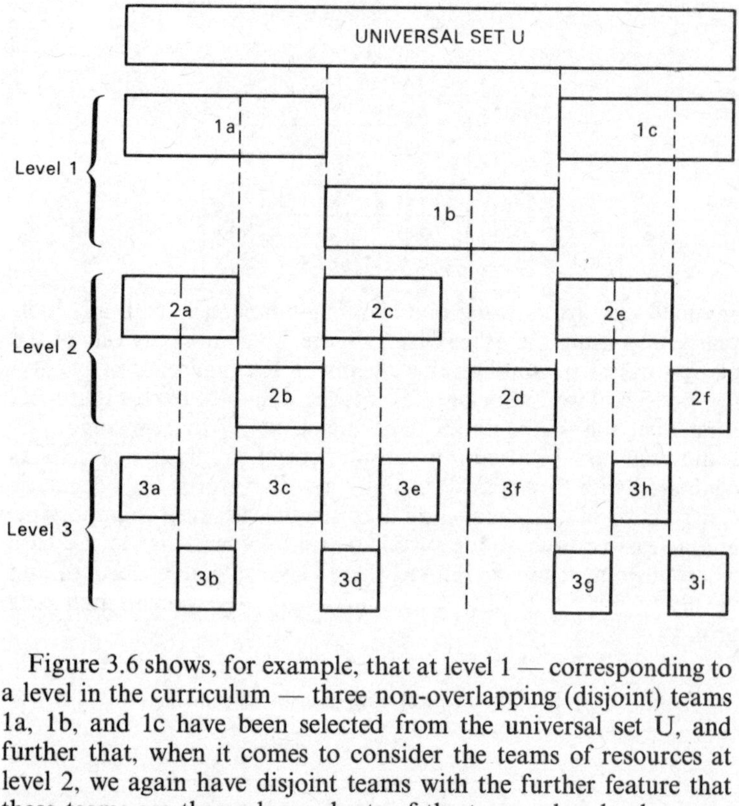

Figure 3.6 shows, for example, that at level 1 — corresponding to a level in the curriculum — three non-overlapping (disjoint) teams 1a, 1b, and 1c have been selected from the universal set U, and further that, when it comes to consider the teams of resources at level 2, we again have disjoint teams with the further feature that these teams are themselves subsets of the teams already chosen at level 1. For example, teams 2a and 2b are disjoint and are formed from team 1a. The same considerations are true at level 3. The Principle of Compatibility is of such fundamental importance that

it is worth spending some time exploring its implications with respect to the various resources to which it may be applied.

Teacher teams

In introducing the Principle of Compatibility we have already touched on the subject of teacher teams. Figure 3.7 illustrates the Principle in a more extended way.

Fig. 3.7   Choosing craft teams

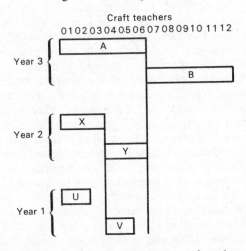

Figure 3.7 represents a craft department of twelve teachers and this is our universal set of resources. At various levels in the curriculum craft teachers are required in different sized teams: at third-year level teams of six teachers are needed, while in the first year, teams of two are required. The Principle of Compatibility states that the teams at these various levels should be constructed so that at any level the teams are disjoint subsets of the universal set: in the third year, team A (01, 02, 03, 04, 05 and 06) and team B (07, 08, 09, 10, 11, 12) do not overlap and could thus be timetabled simultaneously if necessary. Similarly in year 2, where smaller teams are required, teams X (01, 02, 03) and Y (04, 05, 06) do not overlap and furthermore do not overlap with team B in the third year. Finally, at first-year level where pairs of teachers are required, we again find that teams U (01, 02) and V (04, 05) are disjoint and are themselves subsets of X and Y respectively. If the Principle of Compatibility is followed then it is clear that the choice of initial teams is a crucial one because it influences the choice of subsequent teams. In the craft example, having chosen teams A and B for the third year, our choice of teams for subsequent levels is partially determined. Whether the initial teams to be chosen are the largest

teams (A and B) or whether circumstances dictate that some other level is taken as the starting point is of course immaterial. If our starting point had been the pairs of teachers in year 1 we would have gone some way already in determining the teams at higher levels. Special care must therefore be taken in making the initial choice of teams.

In many practical cases it will not be possible to form completely compatible teams: staff and teaching situations do not always lend themselves to the neat mathematical requirements of the Principle of Compatibility. The importance of the Principle is however that it helps the timetabler, and the heads of department, to understand and evaluate the effects of their particular resource requirements and thus enables them to work towards a more consistent and logical approach to resource planning.

So far we have been discussing teacher teams in what is perhaps a rather artificial way. In practice it will often be impossible to stick rigidly to the Principle of Compatibility either for sound educational reasons or due to some imbalance in the distribution of resources. In the first place it is essential to realize, that, of course, sound educational reasons must not be abandoned *simply* for the sake of timetabling expediency. What is important is that both timetabler and heads of department must be aware of the constraints imposed on timetable construction by 'sound educational reasons'. The main question here is whether the educational requirements can be satisfied in a way more consistent with the Principle of Compatibility and in many cases careful consideration will show that one can go a long way in this direction.

Fig. 3.8   Are teams of four really necessary?

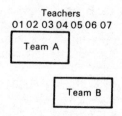

A further problem, that of imbalance in distribution of resources, is perhaps rather harder to tackle. If, for example, a department consists of seven members of staff it is quite impossible to construct disjoint teams of four, as is shown in Figure 3.8. The question posed here is of a more fundamental nature — are teams of four really necessary in the first place?

Applications of the Principle of Compatibility

We have so far considered the Principle of Compatibility only in the context of departmental teacher teams. Its relevance is very much wider than this and it will be useful next to consider other areas where this fundamental rule can be applied.

Class combinations

The class or pupil group is one of the basic resources of the timetable although it is perhaps easier to think of it as an entity to which other resources — teachers, time, rooms — are allocated rather than as a resource that is itself allocated to the timetable. Classes are brought together to form larger units to serve many curricular objectives. Any form of subject setting, for example, requires classes to be grouped together so that pupils can be taught in subgroups that may not be identical in composition to the registration or class group. Similarly craft subjects often require a group of classes to be split into several subject groups to reduce the size of group taught by any one craft teacher or to give pupils a choice of subject. And option schemes too require, by definition, the splitting of several class units into subject groups. A simple example of class combinations is shown in Figure 3.9.

Fig. 3.9   Class combinations

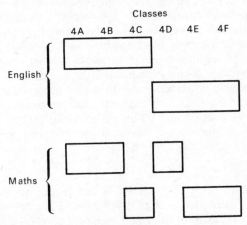

Here, we see that, for English the six fourth-year classes are taught in half-year groups 4A + 4B + 4C and 4D + 4E + 4F. Maths on the other hand, although taught to half-year groups, has a different set of classes — 4A + 4B + 4D and 4C + 4E + 4F. Since the English groupings and the maths groupings have at least one class in common we are unable to timetable maths and English at the same time. The class combinations are overlapping and it is precisely this that causes the difficulty. Figure 3.10 shows class combinations that are constructed according to the Principle of Compatibility, i.e., that are disjoint.

Fig. 3.10   Disjoint class combinations

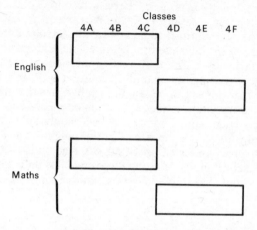

Both the maths and English departments in the Figure 3.9 example may be able to defend their respective schemes with legitimate educational reasoning. The fact remains however, that insistence on overlapping class combinations is bound to mean a harder task for the timetabler who should thus strive to reconcile such incompatibilities and work towards disjoint class combinations wherever possible. Whether or not he is able to implement disjoint class combinations, it is very important for him to be aware of the problems that overlapping combinations may create. It may of course turn out that even a limited degree of incompatibility will preclude construction of a timetable.

Time

The curriculum cycle of a school is not a continuous series of periods. The 'week' is first of all divided into a number of days and these days by breaks into still smaller units of time. Obvious though this is, it is surprising how often the consequences of such divisions are overlooked. Applied to time itself, the Principle of Compatibility simply states that the units of time allocated to any resource must be compatible with the pattern of the curriculum cycle. This is especially important in cases where resources are frequently used in multiple periods — doubles, triples, quadruples, etc. — and where the resources themselves are highly utilized. Again, an example will show what is meant.

In a given school there is a single woodwork shop and it is required for 40/40 periods. At a superficial level one might suppose that 100 per cent usage of a resource is not out of the question. But if this is to be achieved there must be complete compatibility between the time units allocated to the resource — in this case the woodwork shop — and the structure of the curriculum cycle in terms of divisions into units of time. In this example, suppose that the craft department wanted to use the woodwork shop for eight triples and eight doubles in a forty-period week that had five days of eight periods, each day divided by breaks after periods 3 and 5. Figure 3.11 shows diagrammatically why this cannot be done without placing multiple periods across breaks.

Fig. 3.11   Incompatibility of multiple periods

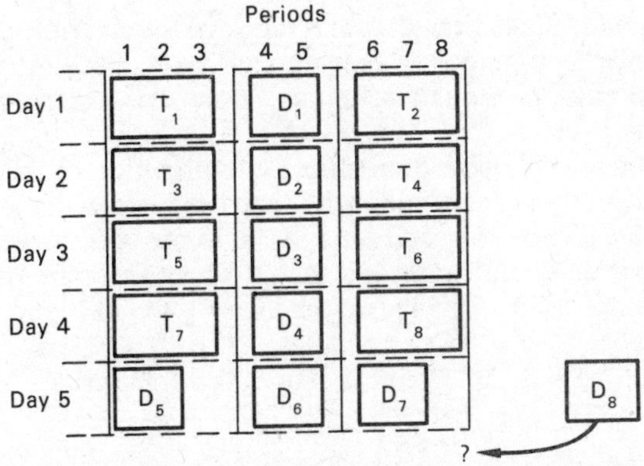

Figure 3.11, quite apart from illustrating the incompatibility in the example, provides a simple method of analysis for this type of situation. This method will be used in other situations at a later stage in the book but it is worth noting that not only rooms are amenable to treatment by this method, but that teachers, classes, departments, option schemes, etc., can also be substituted. In more general terms we can say that for a given resource, or combination of resources, and for a given structure of curriculum cycle, there is a particular set of combinations of multiple periods that will provide compatibility. Such a set of compatible combinations is shown in Figure 3.12.

Below five doubles the situation becomes uninteresting, but the table shows that, for a 3–2–3-day five-day week, a series of combinations will give complete compatibility at 100 per cent usage. The compatibility for any other usage (less than 100 per cent!) can of course be derived from the table. If, for example, a science labora-

Fig. 3.12   Compatible multiple period combinations

Triples	Doubles	Singles
0	15	10
1	14	9
2	13	8
3	12	7
4	11	6
5	10	5
6	9	4
7	8	3
8	7	2
9	6	1
10	5	0

40-period week
3-2-3 day

tory is used for 36/40 periods and is required for six triples, we know by reference to Figure 3.12 that we can have a maximum of nine doubles. Similar tables can, of course, be constructed for any type of curriculum cycle.

A second and perhaps more direct interpretation of the Principle of Compatibility in connection with time has to do with the relationship between various year levels, or divisions within year levels, especially in the senior part of a school where there are often large option blocks. Consider the two schemes shown in Figure 3.13.

Fig. 3.13   Two ways of using basic time units

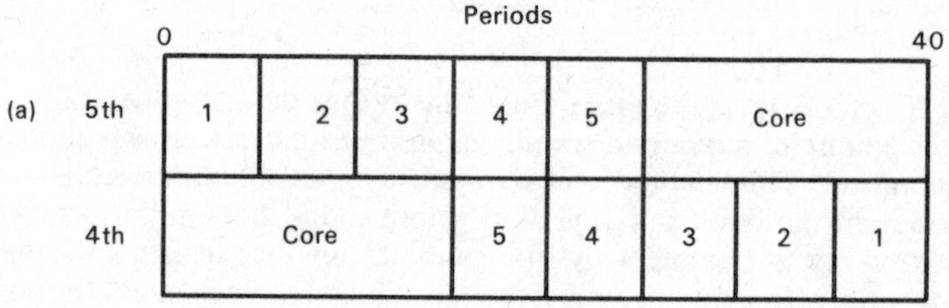

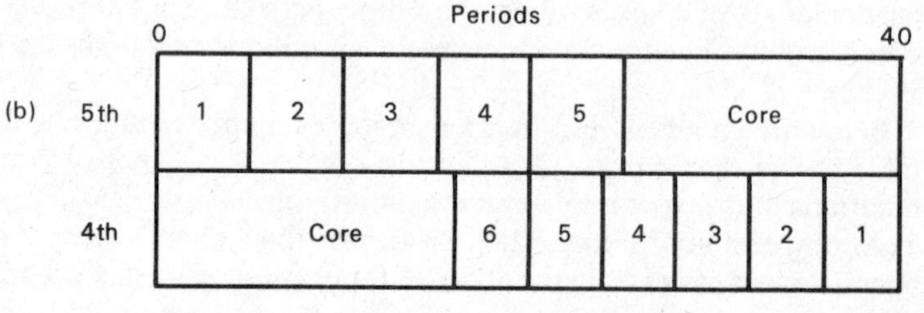

In this figure we have a diagrammatic representation of the curriculum for a fourth and a fifth year. In (a) we see that the basic unit of time for both years is a five-period block — the two years are compatible with respect to their block size. In (b) we have the fifth year as in (a) with a unit of five, while in the fourth year we have a four-period unit. The important consequence of this incompatibility in (b) is that the probability of conflicts between the two years, and hence the likely difficulty of constructing a timetable, is increased: in (b) it is necessary for at least three of the fourth-year options to 'fit' against fifth-year options to give the necessary overlap of nine periods, whereas in (a) only two of the options need to 'fit' to give the necessary overlap.

Incompatibility of the kind shown in (b) is frequently due to the introduction of a new curricular idea, in our example a desire perhaps to offer the possibility of taking more subjects to 'O' or CSE levels in year 4. One clearly cannot ignore such innovations, but it is sensible for the timetabler to be aware that such basic structural incompatibilities as those shown in Figure 3.13 (b) can be at the root of many timetabling problems.

The idea of compatibility of time units is taken to its logical conclusion by 'consistent blocking', an approach to timetabling favoured by some. This approach undoubtedly makes timetabling almost a trivial task provided that careful thought is given initially to the curriculum structure. The benefits of consistent blocking are obvious from a timetabling point of view, but what is very much more open to discussion are the necessary restrictions it imposes on the curriculum itself, more particularly at the senior levels. Such discussion is not however within the scope of this book.

Options and departments

To continue the discussion about the Principle of Compatibility we return to teacher teams. Experience of some hundreds of secondary school timetables suggests that insufficient attention to the construction of 'sensible' teacher teams is the cause of a high proportion of timetabling problems, so leaning a little hard on the teacher can perhaps be excused! In most secondary schools there is a basic conflict between the structures at senior level — fourth year and upwards — and the structures in the lower part of the school. This conflict is perhaps unavoidable since the philosophy behind it seems firmly entrenched. At senior levels option schemes of one kind or another tend to dominate the curriculum. Most option schemes are designed — or evolve — to offer pupils a choice of subjects and thus draw on many departments for their teaching resources: an option offering a choice of French *or* geography *or* physics *or* art *or* religious education will need staff from each of these departments. At lower levels in the school we tend to find a departmentally-based structure dominating — setting for languages and science, team-teaching for humanities, blocking of subjects for craft, and so on.

The inherent conflict then is between a multi-disciplinary and a departmental organization. The Principle of Compatibility can help to reduce this conflict just as it helps to preserve flexibility within a single department. As an illustration consider the alternative allocations of staff shown in Figure 3.14.

Fig. 3.14 Option and departmental teams

(a)

Teachers

	Geog.				French						Physics						
	16	15	14	13	12	11	10	09	08	07	06	05	04	03	02	01	
			X	X				X	X	X				X	X	X	5th option 1
	X	X			X	X	X				X	X	X				4th option 1
											X	X	X				3rd Physics
					X	X	X										French
	X	X															Geog.
														X	X	X	2nd Physics
								X	X	X							French
			X	X													Geog.

(b)

Teachers

16	15	14	13	12	11	10	09	08	07	06	05	04	03	02	01	
		X	X				X	X	X				X	X	X	5th option 1
X			X			X		X			X	X	X			4th option 1
										X		X			X	3rd Physics
						X	X		X							French
X		X														Geog.
										X	X			X		2nd Physics
				X		X	X									French
	X	X														Geog.

In Figure 3.14 (a) we have an allocation of staff to the options in years 4 and 5 and to the sets in years 2 and 3 that follows the Principle of Compatibility. This enables us, if necessary, to timetable simultaneously the fifth- and fourth-year options, or any of the third-year sets with the fifth year, and any of the second-year sets with the fourth year. This is simply because the teams allocated are disjoint, i.e., non-overlapping. When we come to Figure 3.14 (b), however, we find far less scope for simultaneous timetabling. This will inevitably mean not only that more periods will be required to timetable the given requirements, but also that a great deal of flexibility is lost.

Choice of teachers for class-based subjects

Especially in the lower years of many secondary schools it is common to find a proportion of the curriculum taught by a single teacher to a single class group. The staffing of such single-class-single-teacher subjects is frequently considered as an arbitrary matter in which, from a timetabling point of view, one choice is as good as another. This is not entirely true, although in many practical cases there is considerable freedom. Rather than considering each teacher and class as a self-contained entity, it may be useful to think of the group of teachers for each class as a 'class team'. Since these sets of activities have a common resource — the same class — it is clear that the resources allocated to that 'class team' must collectively be able to cover the periods of the week devoted to class-based teaching.

If all classes were taught in this way the problem of timetabling would be relatively uninteresting. As it is, however, class-based teaching must be considered in conjunction with option schemes and setting arrangements. In this context the choice of teachers for a given set of class-based subjects becomes an important matter. An extreme, and therefore probably unrealistic, example is shown in Figure 3.15.

Here we see that none of the subjects for class 1B except PE and Games can be timetabled simultaneously with fifth-form option A because the option team and the 'class team' overlap to such an extent. As a general conclusion then, the teams of teachers allocated to class-based subjects for a given class should be chosen from many different option teams, the overlap with any one option team thus being kept to a minimum. A logical extension of this idea is to have a separate staff for upper and lower schools wherever this is possible. Interestingly enough this device is employed by some schools where the location of separate buildings imposes problems of travel for staff, although in general terms most schools see such a system as educationally undesirable.

Part-time staff

Few schools are not blessed with a handful of part-time teachers. While doubtless the part-timer can be very real asset, it is important for the timetabler to be aware of the painful consequences that can result if part-timers are allocated in a haphazard way. For example, I have not infrequently found cases where part-timers with mutually exclusive availabilities are required to teach together: at one school there were two part-time music teachers, one available only in the mornings, and one only in the afternoons of each day. The music

Fig. 3.15   Class 'team'

Teachers	5th option A	1B Maths	English	French	Physics	Chemistry	Geography	History	R.E.	Music	Art	P.E.	Games
01	X				X								
02	X												
03	X												
04	X					X							
05	X												
06	X			X									
07	X												
08	X						X						
09	X												
10	X							X					
11	X								X				
12	X									X			
13	X										X		
14	X												
15	X												
16	X												
17	X	X											
18	X		X										
19												X	
20													X
21													X
22													X
23													X

department had asked for these two teachers to appear together in several teams. (A clear case for educating heads of department!)

Silly though this obvious case may seem, it does highlight an important point: that the constraints imposed by part-timers are additive when they are allocated to the same teacher teams. Figure 3.16 shows an example.

Here we have illustrated two part-time teachers: teacher 01 is not available on Monday or Tuesday, while teacher 02 is not available on Friday. If teachers 01 and 02 are allocated to the same team, in an option group for example, then that team is confined to the part of the week where 01 *and* 02 are in school — to Wednesday and

Fig. 3.16   Additive effect of constraints

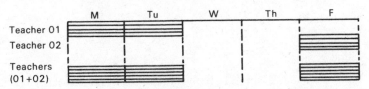

Thursday in the example. Furthermore this combined restriction is imposed on all other members of the team whether or not they are full- or part-time. Such constraints can be particularly damaging in subjects that traditionally require a reasonable distribution of time throughout the week — mathematics, English, languages, etc. — and here it is very important to be aware of the additive nature of constraints imposed by part-time staff.

Poor distribution — 'bunching' — of lessons is a feature of many timetables in which part-time staff play a significant part. This is usually because the constraints imposed by part-timers are imposed not only on the teams where they play an active part, but also in parts of the timetable where they do not figure at all. The example already quoted in Figure 3.16 can be extended a little to illustrate. Suppose teachers 01 and 02 are combined as a part of a larger team in option A in year 5. Suppose further that in year 4 there is also an option scheme, and that only one option, option B, can be timetabled at the same time as option A in year 5. Since option B in year 4 conflicts with everything in year 5 except option A, and since option A in year 5 can only be timetabled on Wednesday and Thursday, option B in year 4 is forced to follow this restriction as well, even though it is possible that no part-timers are involved in the team. This situation is shown in Figure 3.17.

Fig. 3.17   Part-time staff affecting other teams

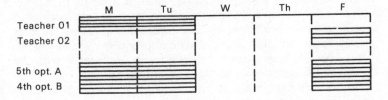

4 The analysis of departmental requirements

In most schools heads of department have a good deal of freedom to determine the staffing of their own departments. That this should be the case is both logical and necessary. However, freedom to allocate staff to the curriculum is all too often synonymous with freedom from external control via the timetabler, and this can be asking for trouble. The timetabler's task is to bring together in a single document all departmental requirements and to reconcile by consultation and compromise any conflicting demands. A necessary first step is to consider each department in isolation and to decide whether its requirements are feasible. Better still to get heads of department to present feasible requirements in the first place. One aspect of this problem — presentation of information — is considered in greater depth at the end of this Chapter but here we are concerned with methods of assessing the feasibility of a department's requirements in terms of teacher teams. This is best done by way of a worked example.

Analysis of a craft department

Figure 4.1 shows the basic requirements of a craft department and the way in which staff have been allocated to cover these requirements. In this example, it is assumed that there are forty periods in the curriculum cycle. Our task is therefore to determine first whether the department can be timetabled within forty periods; and second, if not how the teams can be redesigned in accordance with the Principle of Compatibility so that a solution is feasible.

The first step is to rearrange the information in a more precise and meaningful way so that the underlying structure is clearer. One way of doing this is shown in Figure 4.2. This shows a simple table of teachers against class groups, with additional detail to show the range of disciplines covered by each team and the teaching load of each member of staff. This in itself is of some value since a cursory examination will show that there appears to be little con-

Fig. 4.1   Basic requirements of a craft department

Year	Periods	Teachers	
5	2 doubles 2 doubles	01,02,03,04 02,05,06,07	in option 1 in option 2
4	2 doubles 2 doubles	01,03,07,09 01,04,06,09	in option 1 in option 2
3	3 doubles 3 doubles	01,02,04,05,06,09 02,05,06,07,08,09	$2\frac{1}{2}$-year groups
2	3 doubles 3 doubles 3 doubles	04,06,08,09 02,03,04,08 01,03,07,09	3 groups of 2 classes
1	3 doubles 3 doubles 3 doubles 3 doubles 3 doubles 3 doubles	01,07 04,08 06,08 03,05 02,03 05,07	Single classes

All staff are required for a departmental meeting (1 double)

Teachers 01,05,08 teach WOODWORK   ⎫ MEN
Teachers 02,09   teach METALWORK   ⎭
Teachers 03,06   teach NEEDLEWORK   ⎫ WOMEN
Teachers 04,07   teach DOMESTIC SCIENCE ⎭

sistency in the teams chosen. We need however to continue the analysis a stage further to answer the basic question of feasibility. We can do this by further rearranging the information so that the variables of major interest to us — teachers and the curriculum cycle — are the main features. Figure 4.3 shows this step.

The rearrangement shown in Figure 4.3 enables us to illustrate the central aspect of the information: the nature and consequences of the teacher teams selected in terms of the total number of periods needed to timetable the requirements. The figure shows that teams (01, 02, 03, 04) and (02, 05, 06, 07) must occupy two unique sets of four periods because they are in conflict — teacher 02 is common. The entries in the cells of the table (5(1), 5(2)) are simply references to the year group to which the relevant teacher team belongs and provide a useful check while constructing the table.

Figure 4.3 shows, of course, only the early stages of the analysis. Figure 4.4 shows the same analysis at a more advanced stage. Here the analysis has reached the stage at which all periods for one of the staff (02) have been entered. It is worth saying that, in general, an

Fig. 4.2   Rearrangement of basic information

Year	Teachers									Periods	Subjects covered
	01	02	03	04	05	06	07	08	09		
5(1)	X	X	X	X						4	W M N D
5(2)		X			X	X	X			4	W M N D
4(1)	X		X			X		X		4	W M N D
4(2)	X			X		X			X	4	W M N D
3(1)	X	X		X	X	X			X	6	W M N DW M
3(2)		X			X	X	X	X	X	6	W M N DW M
2(1)				X		X		X	X	6	W M N D
2(2)	X		X	X				X		6	W M N D
2(3)	X		X				X		X	6	W M N D
1(1)	X						X			6	
1(2)			X				X			6	
1(3)					X		X			6	
1(4)			X	X						6	1 MAN + 1 WOMAN
1(5)		X	X							6	
1(6)				X		X				6	
MEETING	X	X	X	X	X	X	X	X	X	2	
Total periods/teacher	32	34	34	34	30	34	34	32	34		

analysis like this can begin with the most critical resource, in this case the teacher with the heaviest workload. Since there are several rivals for this claim in the present example, the choice of starting point is necessarily arbitrary although it is worth noting that both the third-year blocks — the requirements needing the largest number of staff — have been included by starting with 02 (06 or 08 would have done just as well). So far the analysis has not shown

Fig. 4.3   The first stage of analysis

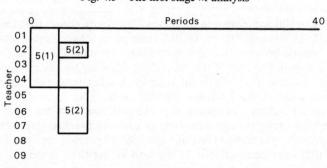

Fig. 4.4   The analysis when all periods for teacher 02 have been added

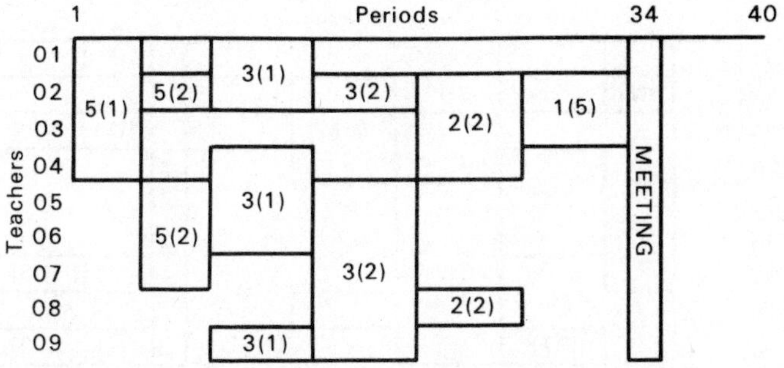

anything especially dramatic: it is self-evident that if a teacher is to teach thirty-four periods then he needs thirty-four unique periods to be made available to him. The next stage is where the process begins to be more interesting.

The construction of the diagram shown in Figure 4.4 is continued by considering the remaining class groups and entering them in such a way that no teacher appears more than once in any period. In most practical cases it is not necessary to be over-formal in defining how to proceed, although several suggestions might be helpful as the basis for a more rigorous approach. Here again the concept of a 'critical' resource is useful. Intuitively we know that analysis should continue by considering the resource that is now the one with most periods to be inserted in the diagram. This resource can be determined as shown in Figure 4.5. This figure shows that, if our reasoning is correct, teacher 07 should be considered next, since he has still twenty-two periods to be fitted. The question here is 'how many of these twenty-two periods do not overlap with the thirty-four periods already entered for teacher 02?' or rather 'how many more *unique* periods do we need to accommodate teacher 07?'.

Examination of Figure 4.6 shows that both fourth-year option 1,

Fig. 4.5   Finding the critical resource

Teacher	01	02	03	04	05	06	07	08	09
Total periods	32	34	34	34	30	34	34	32	34
Periods complete	12	34	18	18	18	18	12	14	14
Periods left	20	0	16	16	12	16	22	18	20

Critical resource now

Critical resource, stage 1

Fig. 4.6   Adding critical activities to the analysis

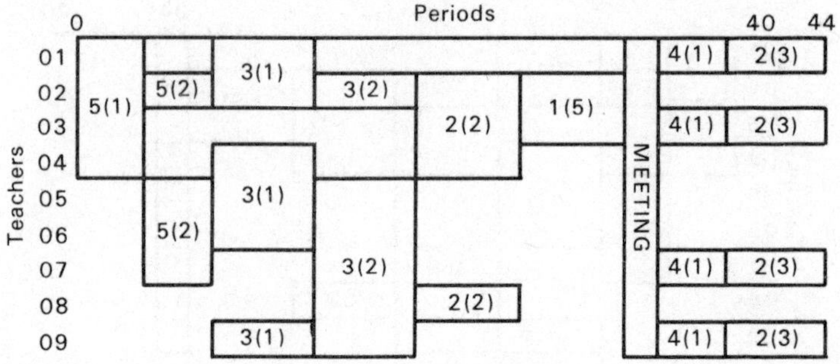

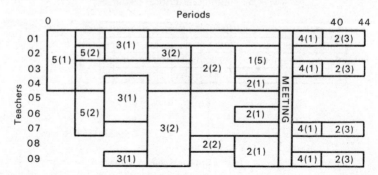

and second year (3) (which involve teacher 07) — a total of ten periods — have at least one member of staff in common with the thirty-four periods already entered for teacher 02. This necessarily means that a further ten unique periods must be used bringing the total to forty-four as shown in Figure 4.6.

Fig. 4.7   Finding the new critical resource

Teacher	01	02	03	04	05	06	07	08	09
Total periods	32	34	34	34	30	34	34	32	34
Periods complete	22	34	28	18	18	18	22	14	24
Periods left	10	0	6	16	12	16	12	18	10

Critical resource now

The analysis should of course proceed beyond this point although it is already clear that a solution is impossible. The following figures show the continuation until, in Figure 4.13, the analysis is completed.

Fig. 4.8   Adding 'fixed' periods for teacher 08

Fig. 4.9   Finding the next critical resource

Teacher	01	02	03	04	05	06	07	08	09
Total periods	32	34	34	34	30	34	34	32	34
Periods complete	22	34	28	24	18	24	22	20	30
Periods left	10	0	6	10	12	10	12	12	4

↑
Critical resource now
(07 and 08 considered already)

Figure 4.7 shows that the next teacher to consider is teacher 08. Although none of the periods for this teacher requires periods outside the forty-four reached so far, 2(1) is added to the diagram in Figure 4.8 because it has no alternative location other than with 1(5).

Figure 4.9 reveals that teacher 05 is next to be considered. (Although teacher 07 has an equal number of periods, we have

Fig. 4.10   Bringing the total to 50 periods

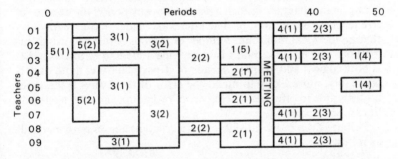

already discovered that only his role in 2(1) is critical.) Teacher 05 forces us to extend the total periods needed by another six because the 1(4) group cannot go with anything already entered. This is shown in Figure 4.10.

In Figure 4.11 we have a choice of the next teacher to consider and teacher 01 is chosen arbitrarily. We can add all the remaining

Fig. 4.11   Teacher 01 is chosen arbitrarily

Teacher	01	02	03	04	05	06	07	08	09
Total periods	32	34	34	34	30	34	34	32	34
Periods complete	22	34	34	28	24	24	22	20	30
Periods left	10	0	0	10	6	10	12	12	4

↑   ↑   ↑
Arbitrary choice of critical resource

Fig. 4.12   The analysis nearing completion

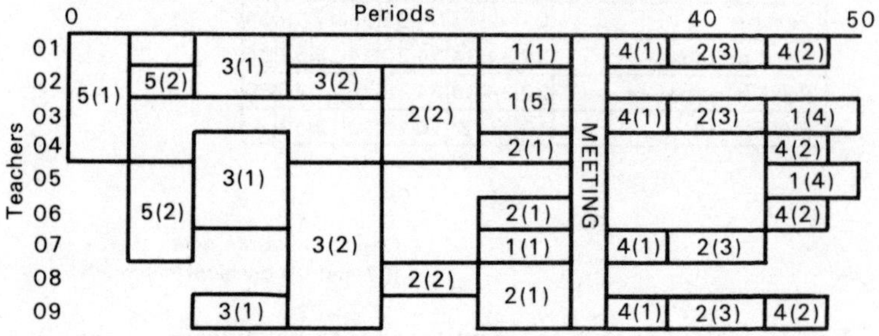

periods for teacher 01 with no further increase in the total of fifty periods. This is shown in Figure 4.12. Finally all the remaining periods are added by inspection to give the complete analysis shown in Figure 4.13.

Other versions, and indeed, alternative methods, can of course be devised. One alternative is to use a method called 'clearing'. Here one selects *any* team as the starting point and inserts subsequent teams on the diagram in such a way that in any period the number of free teachers is a minimum. The interested reader may care to verify that an identical minimum number of periods is reached using this method. The essential point is to provide a method of analysis that is both logical and graphic. Heads of department are, quite understandably, more likely to mend the error of their ways if the timetabler is able to offer convincing proof rather than stating mystically 'it can't be done!'

Perhaps even more satisfactory is a combination of both methods as follows:

1. Find a mutually conflicting set of activities (i.e. a set in which each activity is in conflict with all others in the set).
2. For the remaining activities select those combinations that

Fig. 4.13   Complete analysis

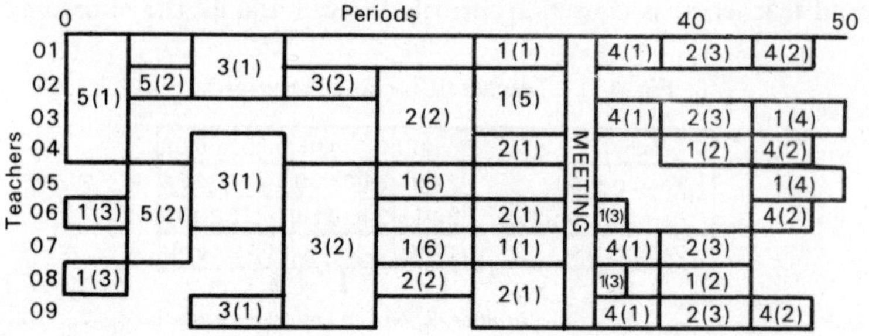

reduce unused resources to a minimum for all periods, beginning where there are fewest such possible combinations and where the minimum unused resources is also a minimum.

Redesign of teacher teams

The analysis has so far shown that it is quite impossible to satisfy the initial requirements for the craft department. While this is of course a useful point to have reached, it is necessary to consider what shall be done to remedy matters. In many schools the need for modifications to initial requirements is not discovered until the timetable is being constructed with the result that *ad hoc* and often unsatisfactory compromises are made. It would be presumptuous to say that a prior analysis removes the need for compromises at a later stage. But at least the number of such compromises and their effect on the quality of the final timetable should be reduced by concentration of effort at the planning stage.

The redesign of the craft teams in the example takes us back to the Principle of Compatibility: this is the basis for our decisions. Again there will be many variations on the solutions shown here, depending on local circumstances and priorities that it would be misleading to invent but which will normally be a major determining factor. We will assume for the sake of convenience that the mix of disciplines (woodwork, metalwork, etc.) shall be identical to that given in Figure 4.1 above, and that the staff loadings shall be more or less the same. Requirements in years 2, 4 and 5 are thus for teams of four teachers offering four subjects, while in the third year we need teams of six. In the first year a male/female pairing is required. Since there are only nine teachers in all, the two third-year teams must overlap and moreover can only be timetabled simultaneously with a first year. Any two teams of four (from different years) could be timetabled simultaneously if correctly chosen, and one could, if necessary, put four first years on together. The total periods required for each size of team and thus an initial theoretical check on the minimum feasible number of periods is shown in Figure 4.14. We now know that the basic requirements — given the right teams — can be timetabled within the available periods. This is encouraging since it shows that the perhaps more fundamental question of curriculum structure is not the key issue.

Let us continue the reconstruction of teams on the assumption that complete compatibility is possible. Since the majority of teams are of either four or two staff, consider these first — Figure 4.15 shows a possible set of teams. Note that the final decision on which teachers are to be in which teams has been deferred by replacing the numbers by N_1, N_2, etc. In Figure 4.15 we see that perfectly compatible teams have been constructed, but that W_2 has not yet been used. The decision of exactly which teacher is to belong to which team has

Fig. 4.14   Calculation of theoretical minimum periods

Team size	No. of teams required a	No. of periods/ team b	No. of disjoint teams possible c	'Theoretical' periods required (axb)/c
9	1	2	1	2
6	2	6	1	12
4	4	4	2	8
4	3	6	2	9
2	6	6	4	9
				Total 40

deliberately been avoided simply to show that considerable flexibility exists even though the Principle of Compatibility imposes some restriction on teams once the initial choice has been made. The entries in the 'Year' column show only one of many arrangements possible.

Adding the two third-year groups and meeting gives the picture shown in Figure 4.16. Here we have a situation in which all year groups are staffed appropriately within the minimum of forty periods, but with W_2 used for only fourteen periods and with W_1 and M_2 used for forty periods. Up to a point this inequality can be redressed by interchanging W_1 with W_2 for an appropriate number of periods in teams of four or two. The overload for M_2 is harder to overcome because a change of M_2 to W_2 can only be made in a first-year pair. All other teachers have thirty-four periods as in the original specification (Figure 4.1).

Since the imbalance in teaching periods affects members of staff from each basic team, it is clear that it can be overcome only by violating the Principle of Compatibility. To make the change $M_2 \rightarrow W_2$ for a first year *and* the change $W_1 \rightarrow W_2$ in a team of four would require W_2 to be a member of more than one basic team. A final solution is shown in Figure 4.17.

Fig. 4.15   A possible set of compatible teams

Periods used	N_1	M_1	D_1	W_1	W_2	M_2	D_2	W_3	N_2	Year	Team size
4	[X	X	X	X]		[X	X	X	X]	5+4	4
4	[X	X	X	X]		[X	X	X	X]	5+4	4
6	[X	X	X	X]		[X	X	X	X]	2+2	4
6	[X	X	X	X]		[X	X][X	X]	2+1+1	4+2
6	[X	X][X	X]		[X	X][X	X]	1+1+1+1	2
26 TOTAL	26	26	26	26	0	26	26	26	26		

Fig. 4.16   Adding the two third-year groups

Periods used	N₁ M₁ D₁ W₁ W₂ M₂ D₂ W₃ N₂	Year	Team size
4	[X X X X] [X X X X]	5+4	4
4	[X X X X] [X X X X]	5+4	4
6	[X X X X] [X X X X]	2+2	4
6	[X X X X] [X X][X X]	2+1+1	4+2
6	[X X][X X] [X X][X X]	1+1+1+1	2
6	[X X X X X X]	3	6
6	[X X X X X]	3	6
2	[X X X X X X X X]	Meeting	9
40 TOTAL	34 34 34 40 14 40 34 34 34		

Practical considerations

In most cases it is not possible to achieve complete compatibility at a stroke because of such considerations as maintaining continuity of staffing from year 4 to year 5. In such cases the redesign of teams is at best a two-year process. In the first year compatible teams can be produced for years 1–4 and, where relevant, for the lower 6th. Often it will be necessary deliberately to corrupt the ideal teams simply to accommodate existing 5th and upper 6th teams. In the second year, when 4th and lower 6th move up, new compatible teams can be introduced at this level, thus completing the redesign.

Further complications can arise when several demands conflict, for example the need to include a particular specialist in a language team and at the same time give a range of teaching experience to other members of the department. Some schools tackle this latter

Fig. 4.17   One final solution

Periods used	N₁ M₁ D₁ W₁ W₂ M₂ D₂ W₃ N₂	Year
4	[X X X X][X X X X]	5+4
4	[X X X X][X X X X]	5+4
6	[X X X X] [X X X X]	2+2
6	[X X X X][X X][X X]	2+1+1
6	[X X][X X] [X X][X X]	1+1+1+1
6	[X X X X X X X]	3
6	[X X X X X X X]	3
2	[X X X X X X X X X]	Meeting
40	34 34 34 32 28 34 34 34 34	

problem by giving the range of experience over a number of years instead of the traditional approach of giving a range of classes in the same academic year.

The essential point, however, is that the Principle of Compatibility should be seen as a yardstick and the method of analysis as an evaluative tool.

Information collection

The analysis of departmental structure provides some useful ideas as to the way in which, under ideal circumstances, information should be gathered from heads of department. In most cases all that is asked of heads of department is information showing which teachers are to teach which classes for how many periods. While some heads of department will make an effort to ensure that what they are asking for is reasonable in timetabling terms, such mortals are unfortunately a minority, with the result that the quality of information provided is often rather poor.

This is not entirely the fault of heads of department because they are seldom asked to make even basic checks and are often discouraged from doing so for 'political' reasons (i.e. the timetabler wishes to retain his aura of mystique). Nor are they taught the basics of departmental analysis as presented in the previous Chapter, since many timetablers do not themselves appear to know what is involved or, what is worse, do not see the need to know. This situation is of course quite wrong and a lot is to be said for opening up the relationship between heads of department and timetablers for the edification of both parties.

Perhaps this is an idealistic view, but on a more prosaic plane it should at least be possible to improve the quality of basic information by careful thought on how this is collected. Not only do we want to know who is teaching what to whom and for how long, but we also want to be as sure as possible that the overall allocation is logically sensible. To collect such additional information clearly implies a somewhat more complex pro forma since it has to be self-checking. This means that the data collection sheet will be harder to fill in than the straightforward type more commonly encountered; and this is an immediate drawback. Against this must be weighed the potential gain in quality of information (if the forms are properly understood and completed!). The drawbacks and gains must be assessed in each case, but here we can only offer a few ideas for consideration. The approach followed in the example of departmental analysis could obviously be incorporated wholesale into a pro forma for heads of department. If this were to prove too much in practice, perhaps a useful compromise would be to provide a form based on Figure 4.2. This shows at a glance the teams used in various parts of the school and provides an easy starting point for analysis by the timetabler. Simple extensions to the basic table could be made to include information on double periods, and special constraints — part-time staff, fixed periods, etc.

5 Schematic diagrams

We have already come across schematic diagrams — Figure 3.13 is an example — but it is appropriate now to give a more formal introduction. Schematic diagrams are simply pictures of timetable structures. They differ from a diagrammatic statement of a curriculum in most cases because they take into account the existence of conflicts between various curricular elements. The curriculum summary shown in Figure 5.1 can, of course, be converted into a diagram (as shown) and it is a matter of personal preference which form is chosen. What neither the curriculum summary nor the diagrammatic form show is the consequences for the timetable of the given structure and any limitations imposed on it by staff and other resources. A schematic diagram for this curriculum would, on the other hand, take into account such facts as whether or not there is conflict of resources between English in one half of the year and English in the other, or how many gyms were available, or how many teachers of RE.

Fig. 5.1 Two forms of descriptive analysis

Class				Periods							
	0	2	4	9	14	20	25	30	36	40	

Curriculum summary:

3A RE_1, Ca_1
3B RE_1, Ca_1 $\Big\}$ PE_2 $\Big\}$ $M_5, E_5, Sc_6, Hu_5, F_5$
3C RE_1, Ca_1
3D RE_1, Ca_1 $\Big\}$ PE_2 $\Big\}$ C_6, Ga_4
3E RE_1, Ca_1
3F RE_1, Ca_1 $\Big\}$ PE_2 $\Big\}$ $M_5, E_5, Sc_6, Hu_5, F_5$

Diagram:

Class	RE	Ca	PE	M	E	Sc	Hu	F	C	Ga
3A	RE	Ca	PE	M	E	Sc	Hu	F	C	Ga
3B	RE	Ca								
3C	RE	Ca	PE							
3D	RE	Ca								
3E	RE	Ca	PE	M	E	Sc	Hu	F		
3F	RE	Ca								

Fig. 5.2   Schematic diagram — initial stage

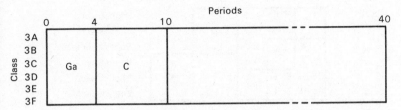

To illustrate the basic properties of the schematic diagram let us assume that resources are such that only one group of three classes can have the same subject at a given time, that only one pair of classes can have PE at a given time, and that RE and careers can only be taught to one class at a time. The diagram is constructed as follows. First enter those subjects involving the entire year simultaneously (Figure 5.2). Notice that the diagram has as its horizontal dimension the periods of the week and that the classes are the vertical dimension. Next we can enter all remaining subjects for class 3A,

Fig. 5.3   Schematic diagram with all periods for 3A added

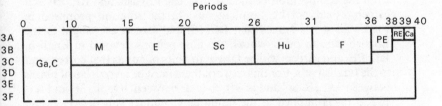

say, as shown in Figure 5.3. It is clear from this diagram that the careers and RE for 3B must occupy periods 39 and 40, and further that the PE for 3C and 3D must also occupy these periods, forcing RE and careers for 3C into periods 37 and 38. This in turn means that PE, RE and careers for 3E and 3F must occupy periods somewhere between 10 and 36. The situation is shown in Figure 5.4. By this stage it is clear that our initial assumptions must be questioned: if we can have only one class at a time taking RE and

Fig. 5.4   Schematic diagram — a structural problem revealed

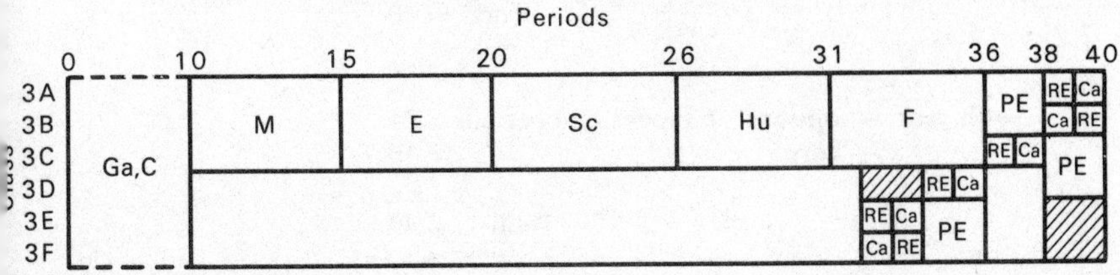

Fig. 5.5   PE, RE and careers taught to English sets

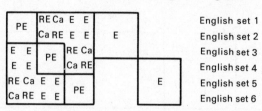

careers, and only one pair of classes taking PE, then a timetable is impossible. The hatched areas of Figure 5.4 cannot be filled by any remaining subject since there is nothing of the right 'shape'.

There are of course a number of ways around this problem; for example by teaching PE, RE and careers to sets of another subject — English for example — rather than to classes, as shown in Figure 5.5. This device is fairly commonly encountered, but may be new to many. In our example we have six English sets formed from the classes 3A, 3B, etc. In the initial plan RE, PE and careers were to be taught to class groups 3A, 3B, etc. and, since the composition of these classes in terms of individual pupils could be different from the composition of the English sets, English, and RE, PE and careers could not be simultaneous. In the solution proposed in Figure 5.5 it is assumed that RE, PE and careers are taught to the English sets. In other words, the nine periods devoted to English, RE, PE, and careers will be taught to units of pupils that correspond to the English sets. For this to work there must be no overlap of pupils between 3A, 3B, 3C and sets 4, 5, 6, or between 3D, 3E, 3F and sets 1, 2, 3 (as is implied in the initial curriculum). This device should be used with caution since the distribution of the main subject can be seriously affected.

We have already seen how schematic diagrams are used in the analysis of departmental requirements (Chapter 3), and we have just seen how they can be applied to the structure of a given year level. We now turn to the problems of conflict between year levels. Take for example the outline curriculum shown below:

5th year: — options   6 blocks of 4 periods = 24
          — core (English, maths, etc.)   = 16
                                            ——
                                   Total = 40
                                            ——

4th year: — options   6 blocks of 4 periods = 24
          — core   = 16
                                            ——
                                   Total   = 40
                                            ——

Fig. 5.6   Schematic diagram used to check basic structure of an option scheme

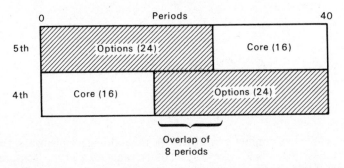

From even such a basic statement certain deductions can be made by using a schematic diagram such as Figure 5.6. It is quite clear from the figure that the structure of years 4 and 5 will only operate if the option schemes are able to overlap for a minimum of eight periods. Since there are 24 + 24 periods of options and only forty periods in the week we must have $24 + 24 - 40 = 8$ periods during which both fourth and fifth have options.

Schematic diagrams can also be used at a more detailed level to check the feasibility of option schemes, not only at two year levels, but at any number of levels one chooses. Such a diagram is shown in Figure 5.7. This diagram, like all schematic diagrams, is constructed in such a way that for any vertical column (period) there is no conflict. In period 4 for example we must have no resource in common between U6 option 1, L6 option 4, 5th core, and 4th option 1. Construction of a schematic diagram such as Figure 5.7 can of course be tackled straight from the 'raw' data of staffing, etc. This approach is however one that is likely to involve a good deal of arbitrary decision making, which is precisely what we wish to avoid wherever possible. It is far more satisfactory to use conflict matrices as a preliminary step in constructing such a diagram, especially where more than two year levels are included. This subject is treated in the next Chapter.

Fig. 5.7   Schematic diagram for four years

Year	0			Periods						35
U6	Ga	Opt1		Opt 2		Opt 3		Opt 4		
L6		Opt 4		Opt 3		Opt 2		Opt 1		
5	Core			Opt 1	Opt 2	Opt3		Opt 4	Ga	
4	Opt 1	Opt 2	Opt 3	Opt 4	Ga	Core				

6 Conflict matrices

The problem of conflict is central to the timetabling problem, and the resolution of conflict is a key aspect of the timetabler's role. Requirements that have a resource or resources in common are said to be in conflict, and it is obvious that conflicting requirements cannot be timetabled simultaneously. In many of the less articulate methods of timetable construction, conflicts are only discovered when they cause problems; when something cannot be fitted into the timetable. By a more explicit approach to the problem of conflict, such destructive elements can be pinpointed at an early stage of planning, and the necessary changes can thus be thought out with greater care and consideration. A conflict matrix is first of all a simple way of recording conflicts between pairs of activities. A straightforward example is shown in Figure 6.1.

This figure shows the conflicts existing between five option blocks in year 5 — across the top of the matrix — and four option blocks in year 4 — down the side of the matrix. Each square or cell of the matrix shows whether or not a conflict exists between a given pair of options — the crosses indicating that there is a conflict, and the empty cells where there is no conflict. For instance, option 1 in year 4 is in conflict with option 1 in year 5, as is indicated by the cross in the top left-hand cell. Reading either down a column or across a row will give all conflicts for a given option, for example, we can see by reading down the third column of the matrix that option 3 in year 5 is in conflict with option 1, 2, and 3 in year 4.

Such information is of course very useful, but the value of conflict

Fig. 6.1   A conflict matrix

		1	2	3	4	5
	1	X		X	X	
4th –option–	2			X		X
	3	X		X		
	4		X		X	

5th –option–

Fig. 6.2   Enhanced matrix — quantifying conflicts

		Opt. 1 DD	Opt. 2 TS	Opt. 3 TS	Opt. 4 DD	Opt. 5 DD
	Opt. 1 DDS	2		1	4	
4th	Opt. 2 DDS			3		1
	Opt. 3 TD	5		4		
	Opt. 4 TD		2		2	

matrices can be enhanced by including extra information of two kinds: first, the number of conflicts between each pair of options, and whether these are due to staff or to rooms; and second by noting on the margins of the matrix against each item the number of periods and their composition in terms of doubles etc. This enhancement is shown in Figure 6.2.

Conflict matrices are not only a method of representing conflict in compact form; they also serve to reduce the size of the problem that needs to be considered. In other words, we can forget about the areas of the matrix in which 'X' appears and concentrate our attention on the spaces. In general terms — and this will be treated in more detail in Chapter 8 — we are using the matrix as a method of defining and restricting the 'solution space' of the problem being analysed.

The most important practical function of the conflict matrix is the diagnosis of timetable feasibility. This function is best illustrated by way of a simple example. Figure 6.3 shows a matrix of fourth- and fifth-year options, including information on a number of periods and their composition. Each year has an option scheme occupying

Fig. 6.3   Enhanced matrix — period breakdown

			DDDDSS	DDDDSS	DD	TT	DDS
			1	2	3	4	5
	DDD	1	X	X	X		
	DDDDSS	2			X	X	X
4th	DDDDSS	3			X	X	X
	DD	4			X		X
	DDS	5	X	X	X	X	

the entire week (English and maths are included in the options).
There are at least three reasons why the conflicts shown in Figure 6.3
render the timetable infeasible. These infeasibilities can be classified
according to the type of conflict that is responsible.

1. Infeasibilities due to pure resource conflict, for example we see that
   5th option 3 is in conflict with *everything* in year 4.
2. Infeasibility due to conflict of time. 4th option 5 can *only* go with 5th
   option 5, leaving 4th option 1 (3 doubles) forced to go with 5th option 4
   (2 triples).
3. Infeasibility due to imbalance of time. Assuming that either 4th option
   1 or 5th option 4 is changed so that the compositions match, we are left
   with 4th options 2, 3, and 4 (24 periods) which can only go with 5th
   option 1 and 2 (20 periods).

Fig. 6.4   Analysis — initial stage

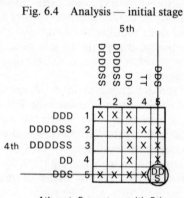

4th opt. 5 must go with 5th opt. 5
(step 2)

The deductive sequence summarized above is shown more completely in Figures 6.4–6.6. Figure 6.4 shows how the matrix is reduced to the smaller matrix of Figure 6.5. Here again note that we are
reducing the solution space by eliminating areas of the matrix

Fig. 6.5   Analysis after step 2

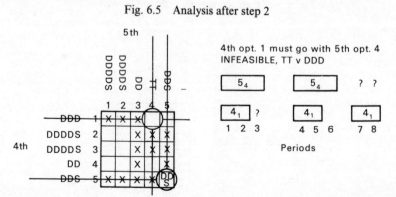

Fig. 6.6   Analysis after step 3

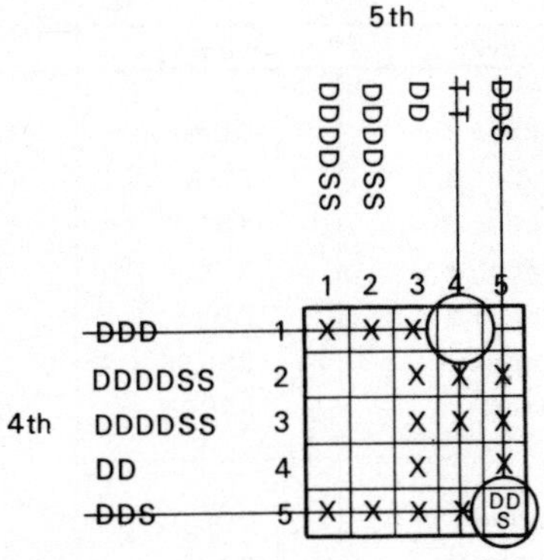

4th 2,3,4 = 10 + 10 + 4 = 24 periods
5th 1,2   = 10 + 10 = 20 periods
24 into 20 doesn't go!

that no longer interest us. Assume that 5th option 4 is changed from two trebles to three doubles. The matrix is now reduced still further, as shown in Figure 6.6.

In most practical situations any infeasibilities will need to be eliminated, and any changes will naturally mean that the initial matrix is no longer accurate. For example, having discovered from Figure 6.3 that 5th option 3 conflicts with everything in year 4, a change obviously needs to be made. Here too the matrix can help by providing a basis for evaluating changes.

The key to the successful use of conflict matrices is in the effective use of deductive reasoning. Fluency in deductive logic can of course be gained by practice, so the reader is advised to take the opportunity of working through the example that follows in order to become more familiar with the technique required.

An example of construction and application of conflict matrices

Suppose that, as the timetabler in a school, you are faced with the problem of assessing the feasibility of the fourth- and fifth-year curriculum. The basic requirements are shown in Figure 6.7.

Our first task is to construct the basic matrix by comparing the teacher teams for each pair of activities, one from year 4 and one from year 5. 5th year option 1 — teachers 01, 08, 10, 14 — is thus shown to conflict with 4th-year option 1 (teachers 01, 08, 10 in common), with option 3 (teacher 14), with option 4 (teacher 14), with English (teacher 14), and with maths (teacher 01). We enter these conflicts as shown in Figure 6.8. We next consider the conflicts

Fig. 6.7 Basic requirements of a fourth and fifth year

Year	Activity	Periods	Teachers
5	Option 1	DD S	01,08,10,14
	Option 2	DD S	02,11,20
	Option 3	T D	03,08,15,16,19
	Option 4	T D	04,09,11,17
	Option 5	DDS	05,12,16,18
	English	SSSSS	06,13,21
	Maths	SSSSS	07,10,19
4	Option 1	DDS	01,08,09,10
	Option 2	DDS	02,11,12,13
	Option 3	TD	03,14,15,16,17
	Option 4	TD	04,14,15,17,18,19
	Option 5	DDS	05,07,15,18,20,21
	English	SSSSS	04,06,14,21
	Maths	SSSSS	01,05,07

existing between 5th-year option 2 and each activity in year 4, and so on, entering these in the matrix. The completed matrix is shown in Figure 6.9.

Our first task, and in many practical cases probably the most difficult, is to determine from the matrix where to start our analysis. In general terms it is easy enough to say intuitively that we should

Fig. 6.8 Partly completed matrix

			5th: DDS	DDS	TD	TD	DDS	SSSSS	SSSSS
			1	2	3	4	5	E	M
4th	DDS	1	X						
	DDS	2							
	TD	3	X						
	TD	4	X						
	DDS	5							
	SSSSS	E	X						
	SSSSS	M	X						

Fig. 6.9   Completed matrix

5th

		DDS	DDS	TD	TD	DDS	SSSSS	SSSSS
		1	2	3	4	5	E	M
DDS	1	X		X	X			X
DDS	2		X		X	X	X	
TD	3	X		X	X	X		
4th TD	4	X		X	X	X		X
DDS	5		X	X		X	X	X
SSSSS	E	X			X		X	
SSSSS	M	X				X		X

start where there is least choice. We can see for example that 4th maths has a good number of possible conflict-free positions, whereas 4th option 5 has only two conflict-free positions. It is easy enough too to see, and even to quantify, that from a basic numerical view there are no apparent impossibilities: if we add up the number of periods in conflict-free positions for each activity and compare these totals with the number of periods for the activity, we find that in no case are the available periods less than the periods to be inserted. Option 1 in year 4 — a total of 5 periods to be inserted — has conflict-free positions against 5th-year options 2 (5 periods), 5 (5 periods), and English (5 periods): a total of 15 periods. Indeed, the ratios of periods available and periods required form a rough index of relative 'freedom'.[1] These indices are shown in Figure 6.10.

'Degrees of freedom' reveal only a part of the problem: while it is quite clear that an index of less than unity represents an impossible situation it is equally easy to show that indices greater than or equal to unity do not guarantee a solution. This again seems to illustrate the difference between necessary conditions and conditions that are both necessary and sufficient.

We have been able to narrow the field somewhat, even if in a non-rigorous way; our analysis of the matrix should concentrate initially on those activities with least freedom — options 4 and 5 in year 4, and options 1, 4, and 5 in year 5. If we look now at the respective combinations of multiple periods for each of these activites, it is possible to narrow the field still further. Option 1 in year 5 for example, can go either with option 2 or option 5 in year 4 in its entirety, or can use a combination of 5 periods taken from both. On

[1] This is even better defined as *utility* by summing only the periods that can be used. In this case 5 in option 2, 5 in option 5, but only 3 in English = 13.

Fig. 6.10   'Degrees of freedom'

Year	Activity	Periods required (a)	Periods available (b)	'Freedom' (b/a)
	1	5	15	3
	2	5	15	3
	3	5	15	3
4	4	5	10	2
	5	5	10	2
	E	5	20	4
	M	5	20	4
	1	5	10	2
	2	5	25	5
	3	5	15	3
5	4	5	10	2
	5	5	10	2
	E	5	20	4
	M	5	15	3

the other hand option 4 in year 5 must use only one of two combinations of periods from 4th option 5 and 4th maths. This is shown in Figure 6.11.

As it happens, either of these will do as a starting point, and we could equally have started with option 4 in year 4 applying similar reasoning. The point to bear in mind here is that, short of carrying out complex calculations (of probably dubious value), one has eventually to short-circuit the process by making somewhat arbitrary decisions and that if, at a later stage, a problem is encountered, we must then consider alternative routes and starting points. This admittedly somewhat unsatisfactory beginning does however have the advantage that it is not entirely random and is therefore at least partly defensible.

We have decided then to start with 5th option 4 and have chosen the second of the two possible arrangements shown in Figure 6.11. Our matrix will now be shown as in Figure 6.12. Note how each step is recorded in the matrix so that the complete analysis can be 'decoded' and revised. It is also a good idea to write down the sequence

Fig. 6.11   Limited alternatives for 5th option 4

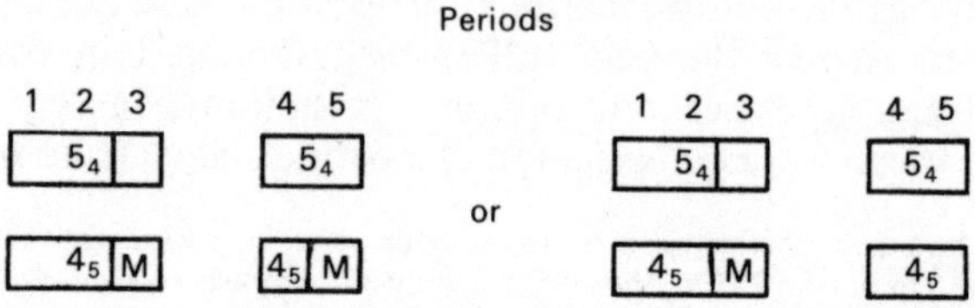

Fig. 6.12   Analysis — initial stages

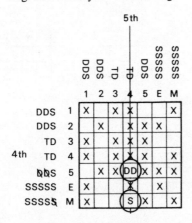

of reasoning so that it can be traced back if the need arises. A suggested notation is given later in this chapter.

It is quite clear from Figure 6.12 that the remaining single period of 4th option 5 *must* go against 5th option 1, and that therefore the remaining two doubles of 5th option 1 *must* go with 4th option 2. The matrix at this stage is shown in Figure 6.13. There is now only one single of 4th option 2 to be inserted, and this can go either against 5th option 3 or against 5th maths. If we put this single with maths, then this will leave 5th option 3 to go with English and maths in year 4. Since 5th option 3 has a triple period, and since English and maths in year 4 are all single periods, this solution is infeasible because one period of the triple could not be completed by anything (except by having 2 English or 2 maths, and this is assumed un-

Fig. 6.13   Partially resolved matrix

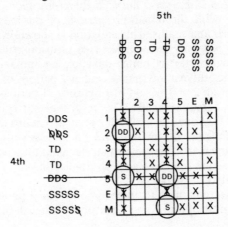

Fig. 6.14   Analysis of matrix continues

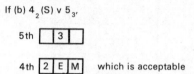

If (a) 4_2(S) v 5M

Unacceptable distribution of 4th E/M

If (b) 4_2(S) v 5_3,

5th [3]

4th [2|E|M]   which is acceptable

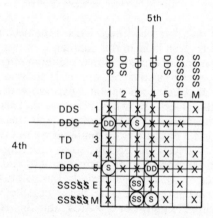

desirable from the point of view of distribution). The remaining
single of option 2 in year 4 *must* go therefore under the triple of
5th option 3 while the remaining periods of this option *must* go
against English and maths. This situation is shown in Figure 6.14.
4th option 4 has only two conflict-free positions (this remember
was one alternative starting point) and applying similar reasoning we
find that of the 5th-year alternatives either 2 periods of English + 3
periods of option 2 *or* 1 period of English + 4 periods of option 2
will satisfy the requirements. The resulting matrix is shown in
Figure 6.15. Only one single of 5th option 2 remains and this *must*
go against the triple of 4th option 3 for similar reasons to those
shown in Figure 6.14. This means that the remaining two periods of
maths in year 4 are forced to go with English in year 5. Figure 6.16
shows the matrix at this stage.

All that now remains is to enter option 5 and 3 periods of maths
for year 5 against option 1 and 3 periods of English in year 4. This

Fig. 6.15 Matrix analysis in the closing stages

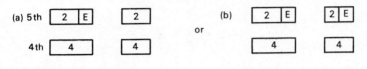

(a) is chosen arbitrarily

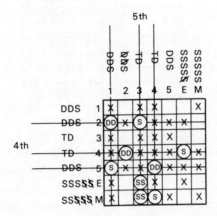

is done and the complete analysis gives the matrix shown in Figure 6.17.

In this case we have shown no infeasibilities. We have not however considered *all* relevant information and our next task should therefore be to determine whether additional information — part-time staff, distribution of activities to days, etc. — has any damaging

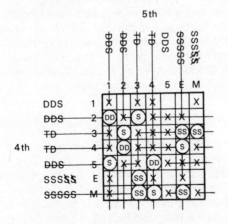

Fig. 6.16 The final stages of analysis

Fig. 6.17   Completed analysis

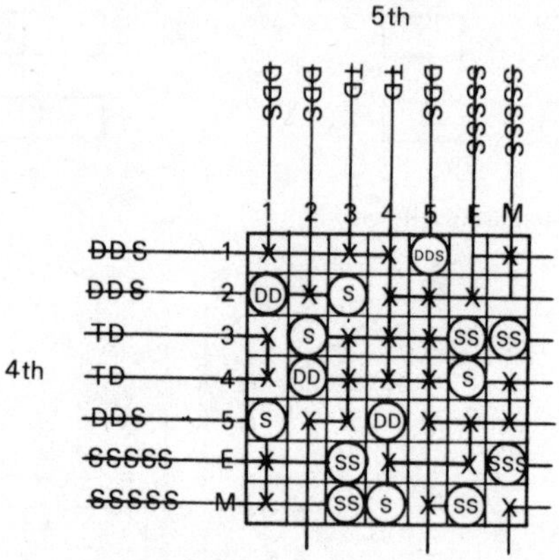

effect on the conclusions we have drawn. This form of analysis is treated in Chapter 8 but it is worth concluding this introduction to conflict matrices with a few general recommendations on their use.

— Take great care to avoid errors in constructing the matrix initially! One omission or incorrect entry may completely invalidate your analysis.
— Begin your analysis by determining the area where there is least room for manoeuvre.
— Conduct your analysis in a step-wise and logical manner, recording each stage as you go along. This will help to consolidate the analysis and makes it easier to pick up the threads if you are interrupted.

On this last point it is well worth noting that, while it has taken several pages — and a considerable number of hours — to follow the analysis in this Chapter, in practice analysis of a matrix should be a matter of half an hour or less and one or two pieces of paper. As an example, and for some more practice, the reader may care to study Figure 6.18 which shows an alternative analysis to the problem used as an example in the preceding pages.

Conflict matrices as a preliminary to schematic diagrams

The point we made in our earlier discussion of schematic diagrams was that to construct such a diagram straight from the 'raw' data can involve many arbitrary decisions. Conflict matrices provide a way of reducing the need for such *ad hoc* decisions. For example the analysis shown in Figure 6.17 or 6.18 provides a very convenient basis for a schematic diagram. Indeed, it could be argued that since the conflict matrix showed no infeasibility, to make a schematic

Fig. 6.18 An alternative analysis

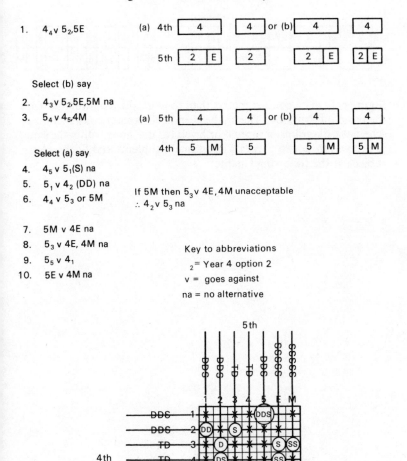

1. 4_4 v 5_2,5E

(a) 4th [4] [4] or (b) [4] [4]

5th [2 | E] [2] [2 | E] [2 | E]

Select (b) say

2. 4_3 v 5_2,5E,5M na
3. 5_4 v 4_5,4M

(a) 5th [4] [4] or (b) [4] [4]

Select (a) say

4th [5 | M] [5] [5 | M] [5 | M]

4. 4_5 v 5_1(S) na
5. 5_1 v 4_2 (DD) na
6. 4_4 v 5_3 or 5M

If 5M then 5_3 v 4E,4M unacceptable
∴ 4_2 v 5_3 na

7. 5M v 4E na
8. 5_3 v 4E, 4M na
9. 5_5 v 4_1
10. 5E v 4M na

Key to abbreviations

$_2$ = Year 4 option 2
v = goes against
na = no alternative

diagram is somewhat redundant. To a certain extent this is true. But there is, on the other hand, an additional clarity of expression to be found in a schematic diagram that is not so readily apparent in a conflict matrix.

Figure 6.19 shows the schematic diagram drawn from the matrix of Figure 6.18. It is very much easier to see the underlying structure, and hence to continue the analysis, from Figure 6.19 than it is to work from Figure 6.18. And, contrariwise, much easier to arrive at

Fig. 6.19   Schematic diagram drawn from conflict matrix

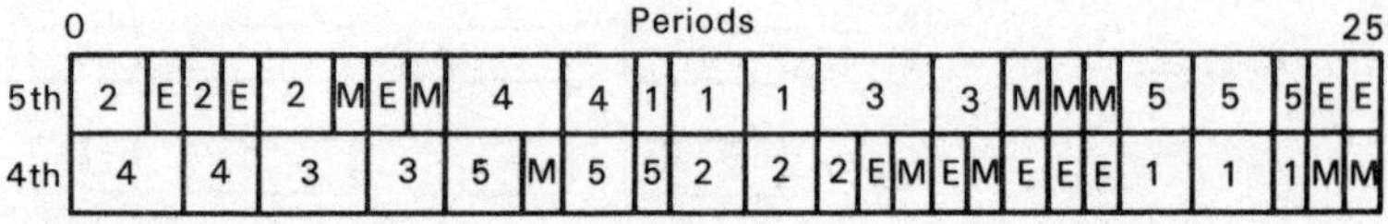

0									Periods															25

| 5th | 2 | E | 2 | E | 2 | M | E | M | 4 | | 4 | 1 | 1 | 1 | 3 | | 3 | M | M | M | 5 | 5 | 5 | E | E |
| 4th | 4 | | 4 | | 3 | | 3 | | 5 | M | 5 | 5 | 2 | 2 | 2 | E | M | E | M | E | E | E | 1 | 1 | 1 | M | M |

Figure 6.19 via a conflict matrix than to work the diagram out from
the basic information. The analysis and subsequent construction of
schematic diagrams of more year levels (or divisions within the same
year level) than two presents additional problems and these are the
subject of the following Chapter.

7 More about matrices

So far we have discussed conflict matrices as a method of presenting the relationship between any two student groups. The basic problem in extending the concept of the conflict matrix to more than two student groups is that a piece of paper has only length and breadth and furthermore most of us are not very good at thinking in more than two dimensions. These limitations can of course be overcome, but only at the expense of economy of presentation.

Suppose we are talking about three year levels, 4th, 5th, and 6th. We now must consider conflicts between three pairs of year groups — 4th vs 5th, 4th vs 6th, and 5th vs 6th. If the problem is further extended to four years, 4th, 5th, Lower 6th, Upper 6th, then we must consider conflicts between six pairs of years. The general case of N year levels gives us $N (N - 1)/2$ pairs of years to consider. This means that we must construct more matrices to start with. All the information that may subsequently be required will be contained in these basic matrices which are constructed in exactly the same way as described in Chapter 6, except that the matrices collectively can be presented in the form of a larger 'square' matrix if so desired. Such a matrix, for four levels, is shown in Figure 7.1. For the sake of simplicity it is assumed that in each year all twenty-five periods of the week are devoted to options, and that every option has two doubles and a single period.

Figure 7.1 contains six separate basic matrices, and for completeness' sake these have been transposed by rotation about the leading diagonal (a a'). For example the matrix of 4th v 5th contains identical information to the matrix of 5th v 4th. Since the matrix of one year against itself is not of much interest, these areas of the square matrix are omitted. All that need concern us then is the area above the leading diagonal — our six basic matrices. But how should our analysis proceed?

Once again our first problem is to determine where to start and, as with the basic matrix, the principle here is to begin with that area that has the least freedom. This can be calculated *very approximately* by simply working out for each of the basic matrices the ratio of positions where there is conflict, and the total positions. For the

Fig. 7.1 A square matrix

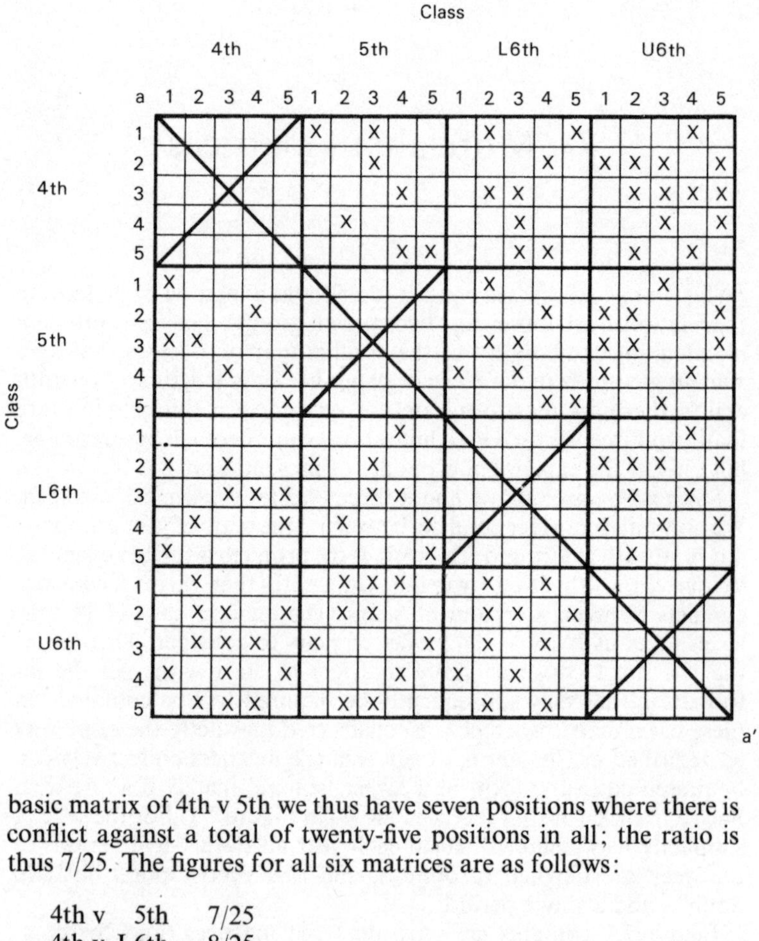

Class

		4th					5th					L6th					U6th				
a		1	2	3	4	5	1	2	3	4	5	1	2	3	4	5	1	2	3	4	5
4th	1						X		X			X			X					X	
	2								X						X		X	X	X		X
	3								X			X	X				X	X	X	X	
	4									X			X					X			X
	5								X	X		X	X					X		X	
5th	1	X										X						X			
	2			X											X		X	X			X
	3	X	X									X	X				X	X			X
	4			X		X						X		X			X			X	
	5					X								X	X			X			
L6th	1								X											X	
	2	X		X			X		X								X	X	X		X
	3			X	X	X			X	X								X		X	
	4		X		X		X			X							X		X		X
	5	X								X								X			
U6th	1		X				X	X	X			X		X							
	2		X	X		X	X	X				X	X		X						
	3		X	X	X		X					X	X	X							
	4	X		X		X		X				X		X							
	5		X	X	X		X	X				X		X							

a'

basic matrix of 4th v 5th we thus have seven positions where there is
conflict against a total of twenty-five positions in all; the ratio is
thus 7/25. The figures for all six matrices are as follows:

4th v 5th	7/25
4th v L6th	8/25
4th v U6th	13/25
5th v L6th	8/25
5th v U6th	10/25
L6th v U6th	11/25

The higher this ratio, the smaller the freedom. From a theoretical
point of view such ratios are highly suspect, and in most practical
cases straightforward examination will be sufficient to show which
area of the square matrix deserves priority. This examination of
each basic matrix in turn will of course rapidly show whether there
are any immediate impossibilities, in which case we know straight
away that changes have to be made before analysis can proceed any

Fig. 7.2   Analysis of 4th v 6th

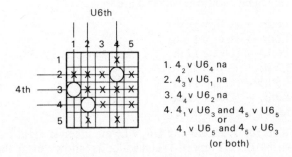

1. 4_2 v $U6_4$ na
2. 4_3 v $U6_1$ na
3. 4_4 v $U6_2$ na
4. 4_1 v $U6_3$ and 4_5 v $U6_5$
                 or
   4_1 v $U6_5$ and 4_5 v $U6_3$
             (or both)

further. Figure 7.1, however, appears to show no obvious impossibilities, although there are several very tight areas — the 4th v U6th matrix shows that there are only two small variations possible on one basic solution, and the L6th v U6th matrix shows forced situations as well.

We should start therefore by working on these two matrices, taking the 4th v U6th case first. Figure 7.2 shows in shortened form the analysis of this matrix and the alternatives available for its solution. The next step will be to evaluate the alternative solutions given in Figure 7.2 (point 4). We do this by constructing new matrices showing the combined 4th and U6th against the L6th and 5th. (Although L6th appears to be the next most critical area from the initial matrix, this may not be so when the solution so far is taken into account.) These new matrices can be produced from the information already available in the basic matrices by adding the appropriate elements together. Matrix addition has its own special rules and the reader acquainted with truth tables and symbolic logic will recognize the following table showing how elements are added together.

a	b	a + b	
0	0	0	0 = no conflict
0	1	1	1 = conflict
1	0	1	
1	1	1	

Rules for matrix addition

To illustrate the application of matrix addition to the example we should first be clear what it is we hope to achieve. So far we have worked out a solution, with an alternative, for the 4th v U6th and we now want to take our analysis a stage further by including another year. Our new matrix needs therefore to show the conflicts between the 4th plus U6th as determined in Figure 7.2 and the L6th and 5th respectively. The additions we need are thus:

$(4_2$ v L6th$) + ($U6$_4$ v L6th$)$
$(4_3$ v L6th$) + ($U6$_1$ v L6th$)$
$(4_4$ v L6th$) + ($U6$_2$ v L6th$)$ and similarly for 5th
$(4_1$ v L6th$) + ($U6$_3$ v L6th$)$
$(4_5$ v L6th$) + ($U6$_5$ v L6th$)$
$(4_1$ v L6th$) + ($U6$_5$ v L6th$)$
$(4_5$ v L6th$) + ($U6$_3$ v L6th$)$

The conflicts for 4_2 v L6th and U6$_4$ v L6 are taken straight from the respective matrices (Figure 7.1) and added as follows, using the rules stated earlier, to give

$$\begin{array}{ccc} \text{L6} & \text{L6} & \text{L6} \\ (\quad 12345) + (\quad 12345) = 4_2 & + (12345) \\ (4_2 \quad\ X\ ) \ (\text{U6}_4\text{X X}\ \ ) \quad \text{U6}_4 \quad (\text{X XX}\ ) \end{array}$$

The resulting matrices are as shown in Figure 7.3. The two matrices shown in Figure 7.3 include the alternative arrangements possible in the 4th v U6th situation. Examination of the 5th v (4th + U6th) matrix enables us to decide which of the arrangements should be chosen. Since 5_3 can only go with $4_5 + $U6$_3$, the combinations $(4_1 + $U6$_3)$ and $(4_5 + $U6$_5)$ can be eliminated as infeasible. The matrix for (4th + U6) v L6 can now be revised and analysed as shown in Figure 7.4.

We have now completed the analysis for three of the four year levels and it remains only to continue the process for year 5. This stage involves similar processes of matrix addition and the resulting matrix is given in Figure 7.5. Analysis of the matrix shown in Figure 7.5, which again gives the alternative arrangements open to us, shows that it does not much matter which arrangement is chosen, but that each gives a unique solution to the problem of fitting year 5. The two analyses are given in Figure 7.6.

Fig. 7.3   Matrices for L6 and 5th against combined 4th and U6th

L6th

	1	2	3	4	5
$(4_2 + U6_4)$	X		X	X	
$(4_3 + U6_1)$		X	X	X	
$(4_4 + U6_2)$		X	X		X
$(4_1 + U6_3)$	X			X	X
$(4_5 + U6_5)$		X	X	X	
$(4_1 + U6_5)$	X			X	X
$(4_5 + U6_3)$		X	X	X	

5th

	1	2	3	4	5
$(4_2 + U6_4)$				X	X
$(4_3 + U6_1)$		X	X	X	
$(4_4 + U6_2)$		X	X		
$(4_1 + U6_3)$	X		X		X
$(4_5 + U6_5)$		X	X	X	X
$(4_1 + U6_5)$	X	X	X		
$(4_5 + U6_3)$	X			X	X

either $\begin{cases} (4_1 + U6_3) \\ (4_5 + U6_5) \end{cases}$

or $\begin{cases} (4_1 + U6_5) \\ (4_5 + U6_3) \end{cases}$

Fig. 7.4 Analysis of L6th v combined 4th and U6

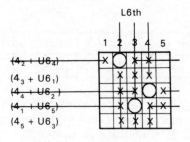

1. $(4_2 + U6_4)$ v $L6_2$ na
2. $(4_1 + U6_5)$ v $L6_3$ na
3. $(4_4 + U6_2)$ v $L6_4$ na
4. $(4_3 + U6_1)$ v $L6_1$ and $(4_5 + U6_3)$ v $L6_5$

   or

   $(4_3 + U6_1)$ v $L6_5$ and $(4_5 + U6_3)$ v $L6_1$

Fig. 7.5 Matrix for 5th v combined 4th, L6th and U6th

		5th: 1	2	3	4	5
	$(4_2 + U6_4 + L6_2)$	X		X	X	
	$(4_4 + U6_2 + L6_4)$		X	X		X
	$(4_1 + U6_5 + L6_3)$	X	X	X	X	
either	$(4_3 + U6_1 + L6_1)$		X	X	X	
	$(4_5 + U6_3 + L6_5)$	X			X	X
or	$(4_3 + U6_1 + L6_5)$		X	X	X	X
	$(4_5 + U6_3 + L6_1)$	X			X	X

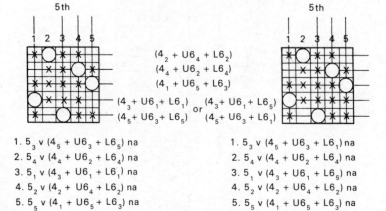

Fig. 7.6 Analysis of final matrix

1. 5_3 v $(4_5 + U6_3 + L6_5)$ na
2. 5_4 v $(4_4 + U6_2 + L6_4)$ na
3. 5_1 v $(4_3 + U6_1 + L6_1)$ na
4. 5_2 v $(4_2 + U6_4 + L6_2)$ na
5. 5_5 v $(4_1 + U6_5 + L6_3)$ na

1. 5_3 v $(4_5 + U6_3 + L6_1)$ na
2. 5_4 v $(4_4 + U6_2 + L6_4)$ na
3. 5_1 v $(4_3 + U6_1 + L6_5)$ na
4. 5_2 v $(4_2 + U6_4 + L6_2)$ na
5. 5_5 v $(4_1 + U6_5 + L6_3)$ na

Fig. 7.7   Schematic diagram for 4th and 5th years

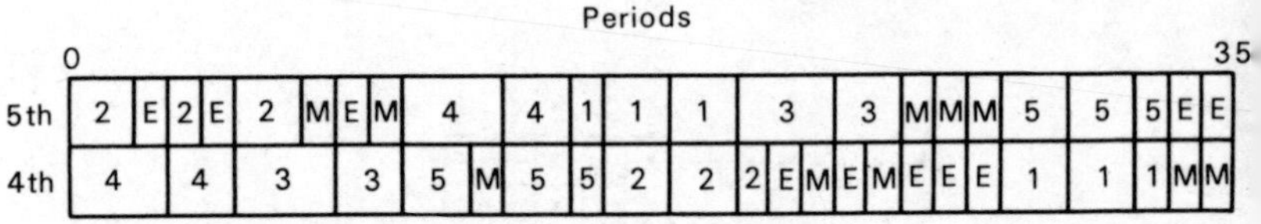

Periods

	0																					35
5th	2	E	2	E	2	M	E	M	4	4	1	1	1	3	3	M	M	M	5	5	5	E E
4th	4		4		3	3	5 M	5	5	2	2	2	E	M	E	M	E	E	1	1	1	M M

This example has been kept deliberately straightforward and simple, but in many practical situations the use of matrices will be further complicated. It is unusual, for instance, to find that all options occupy the same number of periods or that the composition of options in terms of double and triple periods is constant. If, for example, we were dealing with the problem discussed earlier and summarized in Figure 7.7 our matrices would have to take account of the arrangement of 5th 2 and E together with 4th 4. This can be done by simply splitting the combined 4th and 5th years into as many *unique* activities as necessary: in this case we need one row of the matrix for $(5_2 + 4_4)$ and a new row for $(5_E + 4_4)$. The basic form of the matrix for the solution shown in Figure 7.7 against another year is shown in Figure 7.8.

An alternative method of presentation that may be more attractive in such cases and in those of similar complexity is derived by combining the concept of the conflict matrix with the schematic diagram itself, as shown in Figure 7.9. Here we have simply reproduced the schematic diagram of Figure 7.7 and have added the activities for the year or years that interest us by extending the diagram. The

Fig. 7.8   Taking account of unique activities

		L6 1	2	3	4	5
$5_2 + 4_4$ }	TD		X	X		
$5E + 4_4$				X		
$5_2 + 4_3$ }	TD		X	X	X	
$5M + 4_3$				X	X	X
$5E + 4_3$				X	X	
$5_4 + 4_5$ }	TD	X				X
$5_4 + 4M$		X	X			
$5_1 + 4_5$	S	X				X
$5_1 + 4_2$	DD	X		X		
$5_3 + 4_2$ }	TD		X	X	X	
$5_3 + 4_3$			X		X	
$5_3 + 4M$			X	X	X	
$5M + 4E$	SSS			X		X
$5_5 + 4_1$	DDS	X		X	X	X
$5E + 4M$	SS		X	X		

Fig. 7.9 A schematic matrix

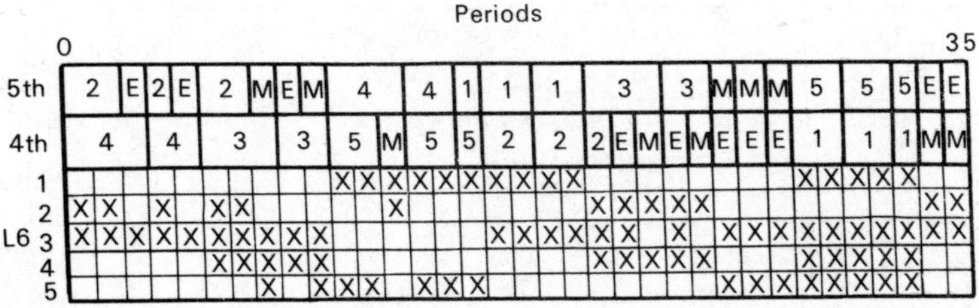

Periods

conflicts for each activity with the combined 4th and 5th are entered in the same way as conflicts in an ordinary matrix so that, for example, L6 option 1 is seen to conflict with $(5_4 + 4_5)$, $(5_4 + 4_M)$, $(5_1 + 4_5)$, $(5_1 + 4_2)$, and $(5_5 + 4_1)$. Analysis proceeds just as for the usual matrix — for instance $L6_2$ is the only activity that can go with $(5_5 + 4_1)$. Matrices in the form of Figure 7.9 are called 'schematic matrices'.

Sixth-form structures

The schematic matrix — a cross between a conflict matrix and a schematic diagram — proves especially useful in certain sixth-form structures where there is no previously determined pattern of staff allocation but in which the basic requirements are nevertheless known. Consider as an example the curriculum for an upper-sixth given in Figure 7.10 In this example there are no fixed teams of staff for each option such as we might find in years 4 or 5. Rather we have a range of alternative teams for each period. Take option 1 for example. In English and art we have the same subject taught by several members of staff (each covering a different aspect of the subject perhaps). We also have a variable number of periods allocated for subjects in the same option — English has six periods, while physics has seven.

Many arrangements are possible that satisfy the requirements for option 1, and Figure 7.11 shows a few of these for illustration. This example is deliberately a simple one in terms of alternatives, but in practice the situation will often be very much more complex. The fundamental point here is that we do not wish to decide arbitrarily which team of teachers to select for a given period, rather we want to be as logical as possible in our choice. By breaking each option into its elements and looking at conflicts for each element, conflict matrices, or schematic matrices, can provide a useful tool for examining this kind of structure. Whether we use a basic conflict matrix or a schematic matrix will depend on the progress and outcome of any previous analysis. If, for example, we are in the initial

Fig. 7.10   An upper-sixth curriculum

Option	Subject	Teachers and period allocation
1	Physics English Economics Art	01 (TDD) 02 (DS), 03(DS) 04 (DDD) 05 (D), 06(D), 07(D)
2	Chemistry History French Music	08 (TDD) 09 (DSS), 10(DSS) 11 (DSS), 12(SS) 13 (DDD)
3	Pure Maths Geography German Latin	14 (DDDS) 15 (D), 16(DDS) 17 (SSSS), 18 (SS) 19 (SSSS)
4	Biology Applied Maths Geology Law	20 (TDD) 21 (DDD) 22 (DDD) 23 (DSS)
	General studies	24–28 (D)
	Games	29–36 (T)
	P.E.	29–36 (S)
	R.E.	37–40 (S)

stage of exploring conflicts in the upper school, an ordinary matrix proves more satisfactory if only because it takes less space to construct.

If, on the other hand, we have already established a pattern for years 4 and 5 and wish to look at the sixth year, then a schematic

Fig. 7.11   Some possibilities for option 1

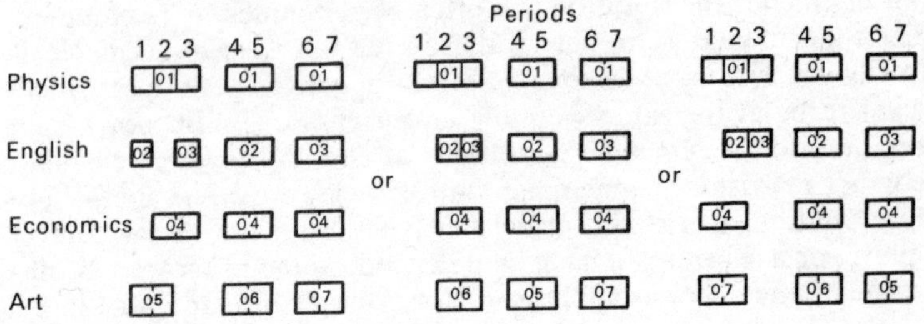

matrix is probably easier to use. Let us then assume that this is what is intended, and take as our starting point the matrix in Figure 7.12.[1] Each element of the sixth-form curriculum (Figure 7.10) will now have a separate row in the matrix in order to show conflicts between it and the pattern established for years 4 and 5.

At first glance this matrix will seem confusing perhaps and our first step is to try to reduce the area that needs to be examined by eliminating any obvious dead ends. Where *all* resources required for a given subject in the U6 are in conflict with years 4 and 5, we clearly cannot allocate any subject from the options that include that subject. For example, the physics in option 1 — a subject having only one teacher and occupying all seven periods of the option — is in conflict with option 1 in year 5 and option 1 in year 4, and since no physics for U6 can be timetabled against these options, no other subject from U6 option 1 can go with these either.[2] Similarly, neither of the history teachers from option 2 in U6 can be used against 4th year option 5, and therefore no subject from U6 option 2 can occupy these periods, even though on a subject-by-subject basis there may be no conflict. This eliminates about one-third of the total area.

Further areas may be eliminated by applying similar considerations. For example, economics in U6 option 1 requires six periods as three doubles, so that any double period positions that cannot be used for economics can only be occupied by singles for this option. Since physics has no singles at all, we cannot even consider this argument, and thus can eliminate for the entire option the double periods that are blocked for economics. The matrix taking into account these restrictions and those similarly imposed by other subjects is shown in Figure 7.13.

At this stage problems begin to emerge. We have for example U6 option 3 as the only activity for U6 that can go with $(5(2) + 4(3))$ (periods 6 and 7), but even this option will not fit without the slight modification of doubling German for teacher 18. We also see that RE must go with one period of $(5_M + 4_3)$ (period 8) leaving us no alternative but to use period 13 for U6 option 1. These forced allocations lead in turn to further restrictions — for example, we have now allocated all periods for teacher 07 in U6 option 1 so that

---

[1] The astute reader will recognize the schematic diagram as the same as Figure 6.19. It is used again here simply as a matter of convenience. The staff numbers used in constructing the original diagram do not correspond to those used in the example curriculum of Figure 7.10.

[2] This may not be the case in a sixth-form structure where, for a variety of reasons, a subject of seven periods has say nine periods available to it. In this case however, we have a 'tight' structure where the maximum periods per subject and the maximum periods available are equal.

Fig. 7.12   Schematic matrix for a 6th Form

Periods

Schematic diagram for 4th + 5th

Option	Subject	Teacher + periods
1	Physics	01 TDD
	English	02 DS
		03 DS
	Economics	04 DDD
	Art	05 D
		06 D
		07 D
2	Chem.	08 TDD
	History	09 DSS
		10 DS
	French	11 DSS
		12 SS
	Music	13 DDD
3	P. Maths	14 DDDS
	Geog.	15 D
	German	16 DDS
		17 SSSS
		18 SSS
	Latin	19 SSSS
4	Biology	20 TDD
	A. Maths	21 DDD
	Geology	22 DDD
	Law	23 DSS
	G.S.	24–28 D
	Games	29–36 T
	P.E.	29–36 S
	R.E.	37–40 S

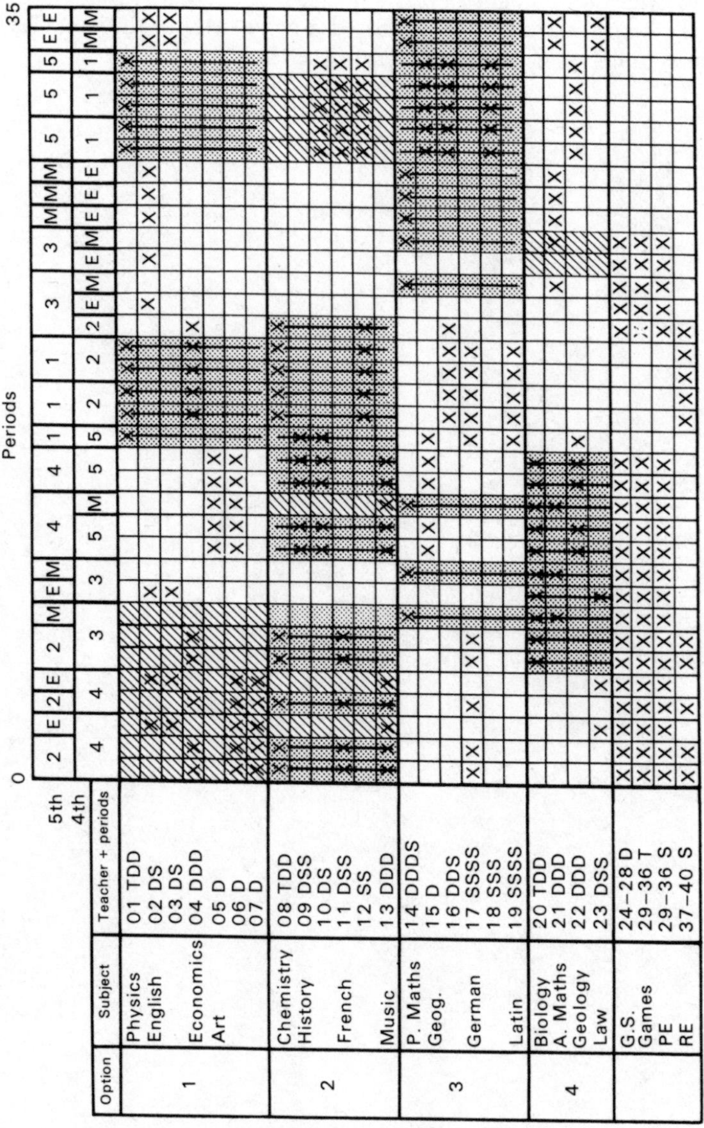

Fig. 7.13 Analysis during the initial stages

positions in which neither of the remaining art teachers is available are eliminated. This again gives a forced situation for U6 option 3.

Analysis of the schematic matrix should of course be continued in order to highlight as many problem situations as possible. Since the logic of such analysis is treated in some detail in the next Chapter it is unnecessary to consider it further here.

8   Solution space diagrams: towards timetable construction

We have in our discussion of departmental analysis, schematic diagrams, and conflict matrices of various types progressed from very basic forms of analysis to more complicated techniques designed to handle more and more factors. We have now reached that grey area where timetable planning and timetable construction overlap. There is of course no reason at all why some or even all the various techniques so far discussed cannot be used during timetable construction. Indeed it can prove of enormous value to be able to describe and define a tactical problem of timetable construction in diagrammatic form.

The one fundamental consideration that has not so far been covered is distribution of activities to days of the week and to periods of the day, and the problems of fixed periods and part-time staff. A simple extension to the schematic matrix discussed in Chapter 7 enables this parameter to be included. Instead of simply representing the week as a continuum of n periods, we now have a plan of the week either as a series of unidentified days — day 1, day 2, etc. — or as an explicit set of days — Monday, Tuesday, etc. In the latter case we are of course working on timetable construction, but in the sure knowledge that the method used is both logical and systematic, thus minimizing the 'hit and miss' approach so common in much timetabling. Such planning techniques will undoubtedly prove of greatest value in those cases where, for a variety of reasons, the curriculum cycle is not symmetrical. The most common cause of such 'skewness' is the need to take account of part-time staff, but fixed points such as games periods, availability of special resources (swimming baths, television programmes etc.), and links with other schools or colleges, can naturally impose similar effects.

The main objective in applying solution space analysis is to reduce the problem under consideration to one of manageable proportions. Indeed this is the philosphy behind nearly all the techniques so far described: their essence lies in a simplification of the problem by deliberately ignoring information. With solution space analysis the process is slightly different because we are not reducing the problem by rejecting information but are treating our material in such a way that the total problem is broken down into a number of separate but inter-related problems.

A second objective that a solution space analysis seeks to fulfil is to discover timetabling priorities. In other words we want not only to divide the total mass of timetable data into manageable sub-problems, but we also want to know which problem to tackle first. One of the most common feelings expressed by timetablers is that they are unsure of where to start. Solution space analysis can often provide a guide to this problem and in cases where no clear indication can be given it is likely that the starting point is less critical in any case. Either way then, solution space analysis should prove valuable as a preliminary to construction if not an aid to construction itself.

Let us now consider exactly what solution space analysis is. A simple example will serve to illustrate the main features of the approach.

An example of solution space analysis

In the fifth year we have the following structure:

Option	A (5) TD	including teachers 01, 05
Option	B (5) TD	including teachers 02, 03
Option	C (5) TD	including teachers 01, 04
Option	D (5) DDS	including teachers 04, 05
Option	E (4) DD	including teachers 01. 05
English	(5) SSSSS	
Maths	(5) SSSSS	
Games	(3) T	MUST BE WED. P 6 – 8
General Studies	(2) D	MUST BE FRI. P 7 + 8
Tutor	(1) S	MUST BE MON. P 5
Total	40	

Teacher 01 is only available P 1 – 5 on any day
02 is not available on MON.
03 is not available   TUES.
04 is not available   TUES. AND WED.
05 is not available   MON. P 1 – 5, WED. 1 – 5, FRI. 1 – 5
Break comes after period 3, and lunch after period 5.

For the sake of simplicity only the teachers with restricted availability need be considered.

The first step is to record on the diagram the constraints that must be taken into account — part-time staff and fixed periods (games etc.). In the illustration periods that cannot be used by a given activity or resource are marked with an 'X'.

A few comments on Figure 8.1 will help to explain what it repre-

Fig. 8.1 A solution space diagram

Class	Activity	Teacher	No.	MONDAY								TUESDAY								WEDNESDAY								THURSDAY								FRIDAY							
				1	2	3	4	5	6	7	8	1	2	3	4	5	6	7	8	1	2	3	4	5	6	7	8	1	2	3	4	5	6	7	8	1	2	3	4	5	6	7	8
		01							X	X	X						X	X	X						X	X	X						X	X	X						X	X	X
		02		X	X	X	X	X	X	X	X																																
		03										X	X	X	X	X	X	X	X																								
		04										X	X	X	X	X	X	X	X	X	X	X	X	X	X	X	X																
		05		X	X	X	X	X												X	X	X	X	X												X	X	X	X	X			
5th	A	0 1,05	TD	X	X	X	X	X	X	X	X						X	X	X	X	X	X	X	X	X	X	X						X	X	X	X	X	X	X	X	X	X	X
	B	0 2,03	TD	X	X	X	X	X	X	X	X	X	X	X	X	X	X	X	X						X	X	X															X	X
	C	0 1,04	TD					X	X	X	X	X	X	X	X	X	X	X	X	X	X	X	X	X	X	X	X						X	X	X						X	X	X
	D	0 4,05	DDS	X	X	X	X	X				X	X	X	X	X	X	X	X	X	X	X	X	X	X	X	X									X	X	X	X	X		X	X
	E	0 1,05	DD	X	X	X	X	X	X	X	X						X	X	X	X	X	X	X	X	X	X	X						X	X	X	X	X	X	X	X	X	X	X
	Eng		SSSSS					X																	X	X	X															X	X
	Maths		SSSSS					X																	X	X	X															X	X
	Games		T	X	X	X	X	X	X	X	X	X	X	X	X	X	X	X	X	X	X	X	X	X				X	X	X	X	X	X	X	X	X	X	X	X	X	X	X	X
	GS		D	X	X	X	X	X	X	X	X	X	X	X	X	X	X	X	X	X	X	X	X	X	X	X	X	X	X	X	X	X	X	X	X	X	X	X	X	X	X		
	Tut		S	X	X	X	X		X	X	X	X	X	X	X	X	X	X	X	X	X	X	X	X	X	X	X	X	X	X	X	X	X	X	X	X	X	X	X	X	X	X	X

sents. First the blockings (X) for the teachers. These are simply reminders of the availabilities of these teachers. Second, the blockings for fifth-year options. Each activity is listed whether or not it includes a restricted teacher or is constrained in some other way. 5th option A is constrained to either Tuesday and Thursday mornings since it includes teacher 01 (mornings only) and teacher 05 (*not* Monday a.m., Wed. a.m., or Fri. a.m.). In other words the constraints have been added (Chapter 3). The third point to note is that fixed activities (games, general studies and tutorial) are blocked everywhere else, their positions being indicated by the heavy boxes. The final point, but no less important, is that *activities that are in conflict with activities already placed become blocked for those periods*. This point, obvious though it is, is central to the concept of solution space analysis. In the example it is clear that since games is fixed on Wednesday afternoon nothing else for year 5 can be placed there. If, as in most practical cases, more than one year is being simultaneously considered, this rule will also apply to activities in one year that are in conflict with placed activities in another. For example, if 4th year option C had a resource (or resources) in common with 5th year games, than 4th option C could not use Wednesday afternoon.

Although the example is obviously contrived for the sake of exposition, it is true that in many practical cases even the construction of the basic solution space diagram contradicts the notion that the timetabler 'starts with a blank sheet'. In this example we can from now on ignore completely areas that are blocked — about two-thirds of the week!

A further feature of this and of most practical cases is that while for a given activity we may appear to have a large number of possible periods to choose from, this freedom is often largely illusory. This is because we often find that one period is as good as another for a particular part of the week. In other words, the solution space is symmetrical. Take for example Wednesday morning for English: the five periods available are identical because each has the same constraints for *all* activities on the diagram; our theoretical freedom of five periods is thus more or less mythical and the actual choice will be determined either by a reduction of the solution space because of other placements, or by criteria that reflect desirable rather than absolute requirements.

The second step of the analysis is to determine the 'critical activity', that is the activity that has least available periods. This activity, generally speaking, should be placed next. In deciding on the critical activity it is essential to consider distribution over the week in cases where there is to be more than one occurrence of the activity. For example, option A will need to occur on two days, the triple on one day and the double on another. As it happens only two days are available, and only parts of those. 5th A is thus an activity with very few alternatives. It is not however critical at this stage, since 5th D should have priority.

5th option D ideally requires three separate days, and there are three available — Monday, Tuesday, and Friday. However, only one period can be used on Friday and this must therefore be used by the single period of option D. We therefore insert this conclusion on the diagram and block Friday 6 to all other 5th year activities. Once again it is vital to stress that, when considering two or more years (or divisions within a year), we would also block any activity that conflicted with option D for Friday 6. Such activities would be easily determined if a conflict matrix was used (Chapters 6 and 7).

At this stage we can also determine that Tuesday afternoon must be devoted to English and maths since there are no other activities that can be placed here. Since we have three periods available and only single periods to be placed, we know that we must change the initial information before we can hope to complete Tuesday afternoon. Several possibilities exist and of course which is chosen in a real case will depend on consultation with those concerned. In this case though we must assume a solution to be able to continue, so we will make one double period of English. Tuesday afternoon is thus complete, although in the absence of other considerations we have made an arbitrary decision on the order of contents choosing 'maths, English, English' to avoid having maths last period. This is in fact an important point since it demonstrates that the criteria by which a timetable can finally be judged can also be placed in a priority order: we first try to satisfy all absolute constraints and only then, and if we have a choice, do we consider 'quality' constraints of the form 'it would be nice if . . . ', 'it would be slightly better if . . . ', etc.

The analysis at this stage is shown in Figure 8.2. It is important to notice that, having entered English and maths on Tuesday, we also block the remainder of that day for both activities to show that we do not want to consider putting more periods of either on Tuesday.

It is now clear that Tuesday morning can only consist of option A and E, and that unless we have the triple of A, we shall end up with a vacant period into which nothing can be placed. Similarly, Wednesday morning must be made up of option B (triple) and English and maths. Once more the order of the English and maths is decided either by consideration of 'quality' requirements, or by arbitrary means. Figure 8.3 shows the solution space diagram at this stage.

Turning now to Monday we can see from Figure 8.3 that the afternoon *must* contain a double of option D since only two days (Monday and Thursday) are now free for this option, and that the remaining period must be either English or maths. In the morning we must have either double option C and both English *and* maths or

Fig. 8.2 Analysis of solution space — an early stage

Class	Activity	No.	MONDAY								TUESDAY								WEDNESDAY								THURSDAY								FRIDAY							
			1	2	3	4	5	6	7	8	1	2	3	4	5	6	7	8	1	2	3	4	5	6	7	8	1	2	3	4	5	6	7	8	1	2	3	4	5	6	7	8
5th	A	TD	X	X	X	X	X	X	X	X						X	X	X	X	X	X	X	X	X	X	X						X	X	X	X	X	X	X	X	X	X	X
	B	TD	X	X	X	X	X	X	X	X	X	X	X	X	X	X	X	X						X	X	X														X	X	X
	C	TD					X	X	X	X	X	X	X	X	X	X	X	X	X	X	X	X	X	X	X	X						X	X	X						X	X	X
	D	DDS	X	X	X	X	X				X	X	X	X	X	X	X	X	X	X	X	X	X	X	X	X									X	X	X	X	X		X	X
	E	DD	X	X	X	X	X	X	X	X						X	X	X	X	X	X	X	X	X	X	X						X	X	X	X	X	X	X	X	X	X	X
	Eng	SSSSS					X				X	X	X	X	X	X								X	X	X														X	X	X
	Maths	SSSSS					X				X	X	X	X	X		X	X						X	X	X														X	X	X
	Games	T	X	X	X	X	X	X	X	X	X	X	X	X	X	X	X	X	X	X	X	X	X				X	X	X	X	X	X	X	X	X	X	X	X	X	X	X	X
	GS	D	X	X	X	X	X	X	X	X	X	X	X	X	X	X	X	X	X	X	X	X	X	X	X	X	X	X	X	X	X	X	X	X	X	X	X	X	X	X		
	Tut	S	X	X	X	X		X	X	X	X	X	X	X	X	X	X	X	X	X	X	X	X	X	X	X	X	X	X	X	X	X	X	X	X	X	X	X	X	X	X	X

Fig. 8.3 Solution space analysis continued

treble option C and English *or* maths (but not both). Since the afternoon already has English or maths, we discard the first alternative. Monday is thus complete.

The remaining periods of option A and E must now use Thursday morning, using four of the five periods. The remaining single period can only be English or maths: options B, C and D, although they could use this period, are blocked because they contain no single periods at this stage. Figure 8.4 shows the analysis after these placements.

The final stages of this analysis begin by placing the remaining double of option D on Thursday afternoon. The other two singles on Thursday are therefore English and maths, the choice again determined by applying quality criteria. Note that we have now placed all five periods of English so that Friday morning becomes blocked for English. Friday morning is thus filled with the remaining doubles of options B and C and the last period of maths. The completed analysis is given in Figure 8.5.

The method employed in solution space analysis clearly has applications in timetable construction as well as in planning and a further illustration is given in the following Chapter.

Fig. 8.4 Solution space analysis at an advanced stage

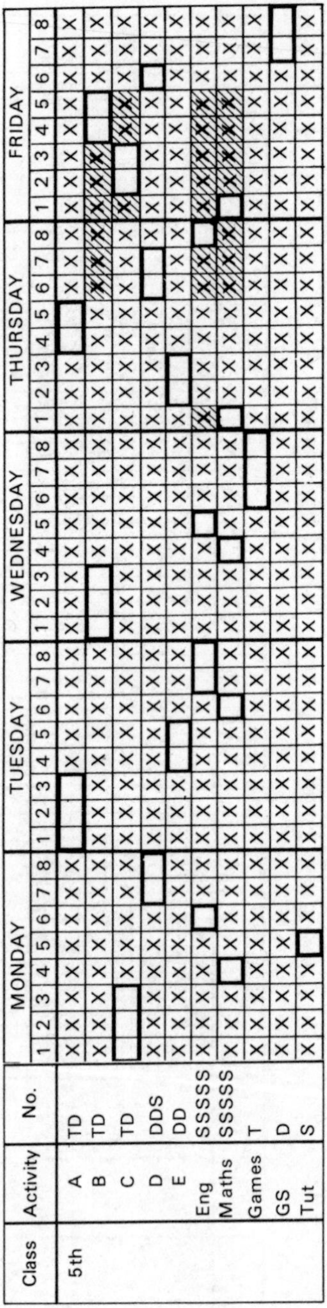

Fig. 8.5 Solution space analysis completed

9 The logic of analysis

In the previous chapters of this book I have tried to describe and illustrate techniques of planning that in their own right are both useful and reasonably straightforward to apply. In this Chapter it is appropriate to try to give a general framework into which these various techniques fit so that an overall design and logic becomes apparent. The variety of practical cases that must exist makes this task a dangerous one since it is tempting to assume that any such framework is presented as a prescriptive model that can and should be applied in all cases. This is not so of course. Nevertheless some general guidance will serve at least as the basis for application in particular cases, and an example may provide ideas for adaptation and development to special needs.

The Law of Parsimony

A fundamental principle that could indeed be treated as prescriptive is that analysis should begin with simple problems with few dimensions and should proceed to the more complex only when any stumbling-blocks have been satisfactorily removed. For example, there is little point in analysing departmental requirements if the workload of members of staff is incorrect, or if classes have the wrong number of lessons. (It may seem superfluous, or even insulting, to mention such basic checks, but experience has shown them to be necessary in a great many cases!) This general principle is known (rather grandiosely perhaps) as the Law of Parsimony.

A possible plan of analysis

The Law of Parsimony indicates that one should work from the basic towards the more complex, and the plan that follows shows a progressive use of planning techniques that follows this principle:

1. Basic checks: workload for classes and teachers, overall allocation of resources, etc.
2. Analysis of departmental requirements.

3. Analysis of multiple period allocation to 'tight' specialist resources (science labs, craft rooms, etc., and teachers in these and related subjects).
4. Analysis of curricular structure — schematic diagrams.
5. Analysis of option schemes — conflict matrices, schematic diagrams.
6. Analysis of solution space diagrams.

It is of course perfectly possible to begin analysis at any stage, and this is always better than doing no analysis at all. The best guide to procedure in a given case is naturally experience, but the plan suggested is robust enough to serve as a general model and as a starting point.

A practical case study in planning

To illustrate the logic of analysis and the progression of techniques, and to reinforce the techniques themselves, I want to spend the rest of this Chapter going through a practical case where planning techniques have been applied. For fairly obvious reasons the school must remain anonymous! This is of course hardly bed-time literature and the reader is strongly urged to use pencil and paper in checking the analysis as it proceeds. The analysis — and indeed the basic data — is of course incomplete because I have had to be selective both to conserve space and to highlight the areas of greatest interest. This is why the curriculum for years 1–3 is only partly given.

Basic information
Figure 9.1 which follows shows the basic information relevant to this example. I have left as implicit the rules of distribution of subjects over the week, since these are normally obvious. I have chosen a tabular form since I have found this to need the least explanation and to be the easiest to follow. The basic format is to have classes down the left-hand side and periods from left to right.

Fig. 9.1   The basic information

KEY	Ga	Games	SSt	Social Studies
	E	English	R	Religious Knowledge
	M	Maths	L,N,P,Q,S,T,U,X,Y,Z	Options
	GS	General Studies		
	S	Study		

C or **A** beside a teacher indicates either Craft or Art respectively
* indicates a part-time teacher

Top section

	E DS	E D	M DDS	GS SSS	S_1 SS	S_2 S	X_1 DS	X_2 D	Y_1 DS	Y_2 D	Z DDS
Ga Q											
26	02	02	19	01	38		33	25	05	06*	35
27	04	04	20*	04	37	45A	35	33	38	34	40
29	05	05	22	05	38		37	35	41	38	45A
30	06*	06*	23	32	45A		38	37	43	41	46A
31	08	07*		46A			39	39	57	43	56
76	11	11		52			56	60*	67C	67C	61
77				53			70C	70C			65C
78											
79											

Section 5

	S TD	T DDS	U TD	M DDS	M D	M SS	SSt DSS / DDS	E		R
5A	06*	39	01	18			SSt DSS 32	E DDSS 07*		24
5B	11	40	05	19			SSt DSS 36	E DDD 05		24
5C	24	42	24	21			SSt DSS 28	E DDSSS 03		17
5D	37	49A	33	23			SSt DSS 35	E DSS 01	ESS 03	17
5E	38	53	34				SSt DSS 28	E DDD 04		25
5F	41	56	39		18	18	SSt DDS 33	Ē DDD 01		25
5G	43	57	41		19	20*	SSt DDS 32	E DDD 06*		17
5H	44*	61	42		20*	21	SSt DDS 35	E DDD 08		25
	45A	63	46A		22	22				
5J	49A	65C	53		24	24	SSt DDS 36	E DDD 08		25
	54	68C	65C							
	61	70C	72C							
	62		73C							
	68C									
	72C									

Section 4

	Ga Q	N DDS	L TD	P DDS	Q D	M DSS	E DDS	SSt SSSS	R
4A	26	13	03	07*	11	15	15	32	25
4B	27	33	38	11	12	18	06*	32	25
4C	28	37	41	25	17	19	04	35	25
4D	29	40	44*	38	29	23	07*	33	25
4E	30	43	53	39	30		11	36	25
4F	31	44*	56	42	31		07*	28	25
4G	76	46A	59	47*A	34	15 (M DSS)	07*	28	25
4H	77	48A	64C	61	45A	18	02	28	25
	78	53	66C	62	48	20*	15	28	17
	79	69C	68C	65C	52	22			
	80	73C	69C	66C	65C				
	81	81	75	70C	67C				
			81	72C					

Bottom section

	Ga Q	PE S	Art D	Craft QD		Ga Q	PE S	Art D	Craft Q		Ga Q	PE S	Art D	Craft D
3A	26, 27	27, 30	45, 47*	64, 65	2A	26	27, 29	45, 47*	64, 66	1A	26, 27	26, 29	46, 47*	64, 66
3B	28, 29		48	68, 70	2B	27, 28		48	67, 70	1B	28, 29		49	69, 73
3C	30, 31	28, 29	46	64, 66	2C	29, 30	27, 29	45, 46	64, 65	1C	30, 31	26, 29	45	71, 66
3D	77, 78		48, 49	67, 71	2D	31, 77		49	67, 70	1D	77, 78		48, 49	67, 73
3E	79	27, 31	46, 47*	71, 67	2E	78, 79	27, 30	46, 47*	64, 66	1E	79	26, 30	45, 46	71, 66
3F			49	69, 72	2F			48	69, 72	1F		26, 31	48	67, 70
3G		27, 31	45, 48	71, 68	2G		27, 31	46	71, 68	1G			49	72
3H			49	69, 78	2H			48, 49	72, 73					

All entries are to scale, but the number of periods and distribution is stated at the head of each new activity. Simultaneity is indicated by the simple expedient of enclosing with a solid box the classes concerned. In this example only teacher and class resources are of interest, but the basic format could obviously be modified to include information about rooms if this was needed.

As a *descriptive* analysis the method illustrated in Figure 9.1 is hard to equal, but it must be stressed that, useful though such descriptions are, they do *not* constitute planning. Also given are various bits and pieces of information concerning part-time staff, etc.

PART-TIME STAFF
06 not available on Friday
07 not available on Monday
20 not available on Friday 5–7
44 not available on Wednesday
47 not available on Monday or Tuesday
60 not available on Tuesday, Wednesday, Friday

FIXED PERIODS
1st year games must be on	Monday	1–4
2nd year games must be on	Tuesday	1–4
3rd year games must be on	Wednesday	1–4
4th year games must be on	Thursday	1–4
5th & 6th year games must be on	Friday	1–4

MEETING
Teachers 08, 15, 17, 18, 24, 41, 59, 75 must be free on Thursday 3, 4 for a meeting.

SCHOOL WEEK
Five days of seven periods. Break after period 2, lunch after period 4.

BASIC CHECKS
Since the information given is only partial it must be assumed that these have been carried out.

DEPARTMENTAL ANALYSIS
The structure of all the first three years of this school — with the exception of games, PE, craft and art — is for class-based teaching. This means that there is no possibility of the departmental teams in the remainder of the school spreading over more than the thirty-five available periods. It could be argued that there is therefore little point in thinking about compatible teams. To a certain extent this is true although any move towards setting in the lower school, in

maths for example, would immediately make compatible teams a high priority. Examination of the present maths teams in years 4, 5 and 6 shows that the construction of disjoint teams for use in years 1, 2 and 3 would be impossible unless the teams higher up are modified. Although not strictly necessary for the present, the time-tabler with an eye for future developments should nevertheless try to prod departments towards a more rational allocation of teams.

THE CRAFT DEPARTMENT

When we come to the art and craft departments however, we find that teams of teachers are used throughout the school, and thus analysis is of immediate relevance. The requirements in these two departments are summarized in Figure 9.2. Looking at the craft teams to start with, and following the general method suggested in Chapter 4, gives us the following analytical procedure.

1. Enter all periods for teacher 65 since he has the largest number of periods. This gives the diagram shown in Figure 9.3.

Fig. 9.2 Summary of art and craft teams

Art Staff							Craft Teachers											
49	48	47	46	45	Label	Code	73	72	71	70	69	68	67	66	65	64	Label	Code
		X			6th GS	SSS			X								6th opt X	DDS
			X		$S_1 + S_2$	SSS						X					opt Y	DDS
		X	X		opt Z	DDS								X			opt Z	DDS
X				X	5th opt S				X			X					5th opt S	TD
X	X				opt T						X	X		X			opt T	DDS
		X			opt U		X	X						X			opt U	TD
	X		X		4th opt N		X				X						4th opt N	DDS
					opt L							X	X		X	X	opt L	TD
	X				opt P			X		X				X	X		opt P	DDS
	X			X	opt Q								X		X		opt Q	D
	X	X		X	3A,B	D					X	X			X	X	3A,B	QD
X	X		X		3C,D	D			X				X	X		X	3C,D	QD
X		X	X		3E,F	D			X	X		X		X			3E,F	QD
X	X				3G,H	D	X			X			X	X			3G,H	QD
	X	X		X	2A,B	D					X			X	X		2A,B	Q
X			X	X	2C,D	D					X			X	X	X	2C,D	Q
	X	X	X		2E,F	D			X			X			X	X	2E,F	Q
X	X		X		2G,H	D	X	X	X				X				2G,H	Q
X		X	X		1A,B	D	X					X			X	X	1A,B	D
X	X			X	1C,D	D	X		X					X	X		1C,D	D
X	X		X	X	1E,F,G	D		X	X	X				X	X		1E,F,G	D
26	28	15	32	27	Total Periods		24	31	26	31	28	31	31	30	32	31	Total Periods	

2. Select the next critical resource. Comparison of the number of periods entered so far and the totals remaining shows that teacher 69 with twenty-eight periods is to be considered next.

3. Enter all periods for critical resources that are in conflict with *all* periods so far entered or which are forced to use certain positions. As it happens teacher 69's periods fulfil neither of

Fig. 9.3   Enter all periods for teacher 65

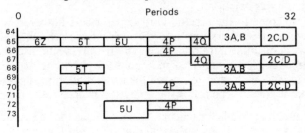

Fig. 9.4   Adding the IE, F, G team

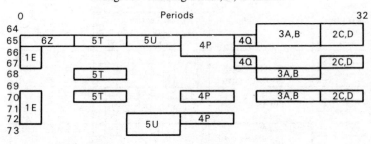

Fig. 9.5   Schematic matrix for teacher 66

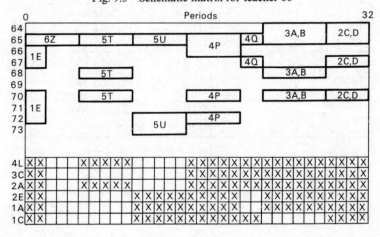

these conditions, so rather than make arbitrary decisions, we select the next most critical teacher, number 71 with twenty-six periods remaining. There too the analysis is not very rewarding since only the 1E, F, G team can be added. This must go with the 6Z if an increase in the thirty-two periods is to be avoided. Figure 9.4 shows the diagram at this stage.

4. Select a new critical resource. Having tried with teachers 69 and 71 we should next try someone else. Either 66 or 67 will do now, and 66 is chosen arbitrarily. At this stage it is appropriate to be more explicit about the conflicts entailed in considering teacher 66 since there are a number of alternatives. Figure 9.5 shows one way of doing this by using the concept of the schematic matrix (Chapter 7).

In Figure 9.5 we can see that both 4th option L (4L) and the 2A, B team are forced to go with 6Z and 5U. Examination of the option teams in 4th L and 5U and 6Z shows that 4th L can go with neither 5U nor 6Z because of conflicts with other teachers (non-craft). 4L cannot therefore go with any of the periods entered so far and must use new periods, thus bringing the total needed to thirty-seven. From Figure 9.6, which shows the diagram when teacher 66 has been considered, we can make also the following deductions

2A must go with *both* 6Z and 5U in order to get a quadruple.

3C must go with 6Z, 5U and 5T (*only* 2A and 3C can go with 5U so we must use as many periods of 5U as we can).

IC must go with 3A since nowhere else is now available.

2E and 1A (six periods) must now go with 5T (three periods) and 4Q (two periods), thus bringing the total periods required to thirty-eight.

5. We have now demonstrated that the craft department, even when considered almost in isolation, cannot possibly be timetabled within thirty-five periods. The interested reader may care to continue the analysis himself and to compare his result with my own version of the diagram given in Figure 9.7.

This analysis has shown that extensive revisions must be made before the craft department can be timetabled. But not only have we shown that the craft teams are impossible, we have also found out that there are many situations where the choice of teams forces us to place simultaneously activities from different years. In practical terms this means that we must either tackle the craft requirements — in modified form — at a very early stage, or we must redesign the teams completely to give greater flexibility. The answer to this decision will naturally depend on the priority attached to craft: is craft the most important department to get right? Or should other things be considered first? Whatever else, the head of craft should receive a crash course in the Principle of Compatibility!

Fig. 9.6 Entering periods that include teacher 66

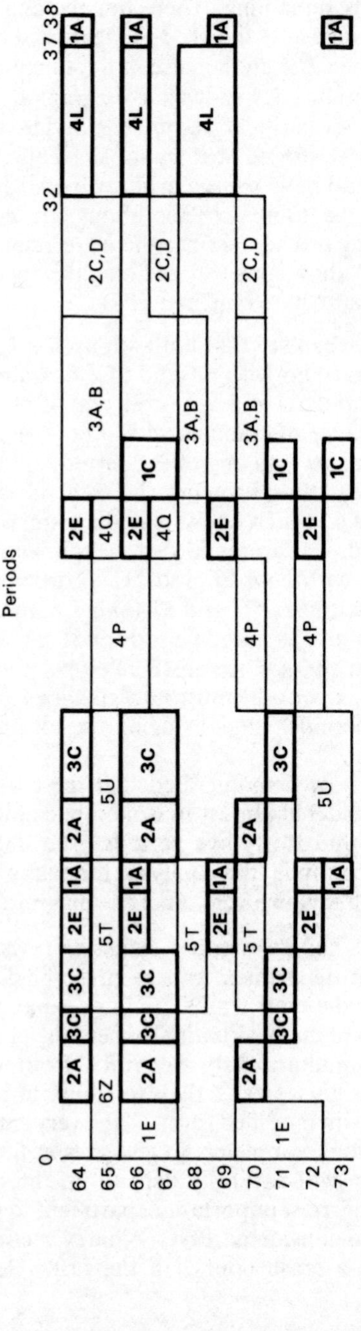

Periods

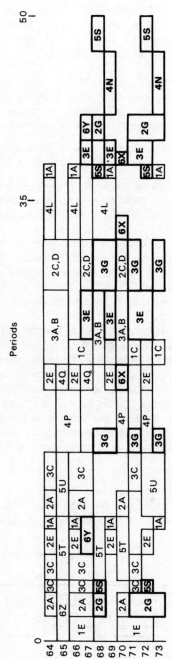

Fig. 9.7 One version of the complete analysis

In this case the craft teams in the options are to be treated as sacro-
sanct, while the teams lower down the school are more flexible.
We therefore decide to proceed with analysis of other features
before returning to the craft problems.

THE ART DEPARTMENT
A similar analysis will show that here, as with craft, the initial
requirements are infeasible. This can easily be verified by considering the requirements as being of two types:

for teams of three (years 1–3) = 22 periods
for teams of two (years 4–6) = 20 periods

Inspection of the teams will show that only one of the teams of three
can be put on at the same time as a team of two and that therefore
22 + 18 = 40 periods would be needed. (One double of 5th option S
goes with 2E and F.)

Because there are only five art teachers, we know that we can at
any time have only one first-, second- or third-year group doing art.
But with the proviso that upper school teams are the more vital to
maintain as specified, then it is easy to see how matters can be
improved by constructing compatible teams. In this case the constraint of preserving the teams in years 4–6 limits the extent to which
completely compatible teams can be constructed. We are reduced to
constructing sets of lower school teams that are compatible with the
pairs of staff used in years 4–6. Here too we are limited because
teacher 47 is part-time and does not appear in any upper school team
(47 is in 4th P but not with another art teacher). But, as is shown in
Figure 9.8, we are still able to use less than thirty-five periods.
As with the craft problems, we here see an important by-product of
analysis — the definition or refinement of timetable priorities. In
both art and craft we have in effect partly solved our problems by
redefining them.

ANALYSIS OF MULTIPLE PERIOD ALLOCATION
Since we have decided to defer the craft problem it would be inap-
propriate to consider this aspect now. A quick check of the art

Fig. 9.8   Redesign of art teams

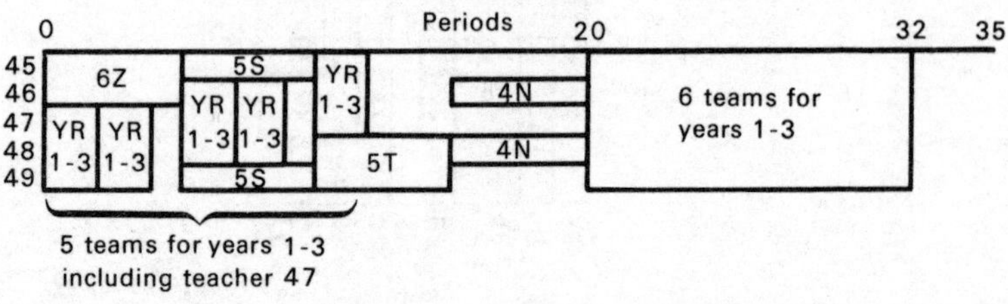

5 teams for years 1-3
including teacher 47

department reveals no infeasibilities at this stage, but we should bear in mind the multiple period problem as our analysis continues.

ANALYSIS OF CURRICULAR STRUCTURE
We now come to a second major area for analysis and in this example it is the fourth and fifth years that attract attention; it is here that the structure is most complex. Consider first year 5. We have to start with fifteen periods of options and four periods of games in which all fifth-year classes are simultaneous. In the remaining sixteen periods $(35 - 15 - 4 = 16)$ we see that the maths groups must occupy a unique set of nine periods because the teams are overlapping. Figure 9.9 is a schematic diagram at this stage of analysis.

Fig. 9.9   Partly completed schematic diagram for 5th year

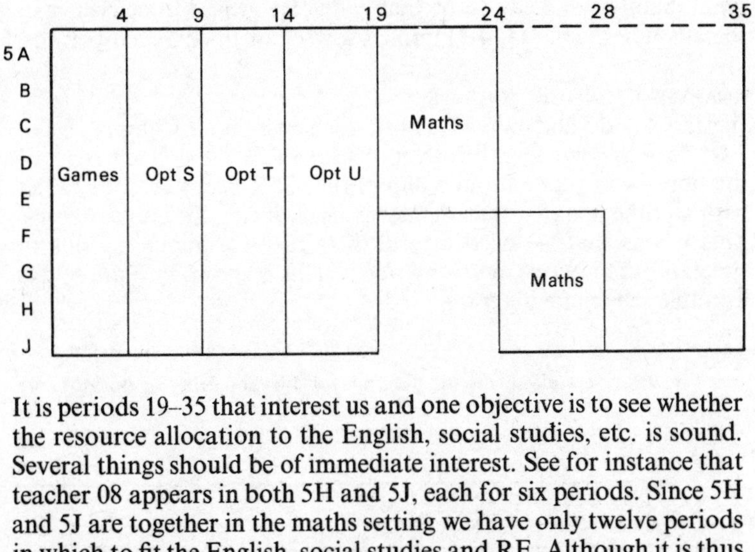

It is periods 19–35 that interest us and one objective is to see whether the resource allocation to the English, social studies, etc. is sound. Several things should be of immediate interest. See for instance that teacher 08 appears in both 5H and 5J, each for six periods. Since 5H and 5J are together in the maths setting we have only twelve periods in which to fit the English, social studies and RE. Although it is thus theoretically possible to fit teacher 08 into both 5H and 5J, it would be an improvement if each class in the 5F–5H group were to have a different teacher for English. There may of course be sensible reasons for having teacher 08 in both classes, but our analysis shows that this will be a tight spot and may indeed prove impossible at a later stage. Similarly the teachers for 5C and 5E social studies should, if possible, be different since these classes are forced to use the same set of periods.

   In the fourth year we have a similar structure, but we have fewer periods to play with — options and games take up twenty-one periods for all classes. Looking for similarly dangerous allocation of

Fig. 9.10   Schematic diagram for teacher 15

```
     0                    21                        35      39
4  A ┌──────────────────┬──────┐    ┌─────────────┐ │
   B │                  │      │    │   English   │ │
   C │                  │ Maths│    └─────────────┘ │
   D │   Option etc.    │      │                    │
   E │                  ├──────┴──────┐             │
   F │                  │             │             │
   G │                  │    Maths    │             │
   H └──────────────────┴─────────────┘  ┌──────────┴──┐
                                         │   English   │
                                         └─────────────┘
                                                        │
```

teachers, we should straight away spot teacher 15 in both maths sets and in two classes of English, a total of eighteen periods where only fourteen are available! Figure 9.10 shows this as a schematic diagram. Similarly we can show that giving teacher 28 three classes of social studies (4F, 4G, 4H) implies a week of thirty-seven periods.

ANALYSIS OF OPTION SCHEMES
In years 4 and 5 and 6 we have option schemes and in Chapters 6 and 7 we dealt at some length with conflict matrices. A simple matrix of the options in years 4 and 5 shows that all options are in conflict with all others, a fact that suggested itself during the craft analysis. This means that we need a total of thirty-two unique periods to timetable the options in years 4 and 5. This is shown in Figure 9.11, a simple schematic diagram.

Fig. 9.11   Simple schematic diagram for 4th- and 5th-year options

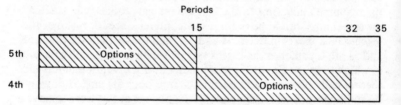

When we come to consider the options in year 6 we need only make a simple matrix, with the 4th *and* 5th years on one axis, and the 6th on the second. The required matrix is shown in Figure 9.12. Even a casual glance at Figure 9.12 is enough to show that there are real problems with the sixth form. For a start, both options Z and Y_1 — a total of eight periods — are in conflict with *all* the fourth- and fifth-year options and must therefore use periods other than the thirty-two required for fourth and fifth. This alone brings the total to forty.

Fig. 9.12   Conflict matrix for 4, 5 and 6

		Z DDS	Y_2 D	Y_1 DS	X_2 D	X_1 DS	S_2 S	S_1 SS	GS SSS	Math DDS	Eng D	Eng DS
5th	S TD	X	X	X	X	X	X	X			X	X
	T DDS	X		X	X	X			X			
	U TD	X	X	X	X	X			X		X	X
4th	N DDS	X	X	X	X	X		X	X			
	L TD	X	X	X		X	X	X	X			
	P DDS	X	X	X	X	X	X	X			X	X
	Q D	X	X	X			X	X	X		X	X

In addition we have the following:

1. 6th Y_2 must go with 5th T.
2. 6th X_1 must go with 4th Q, leaving 6th X_2 to go with 4th L. There are three periods of 6th X_1 and only two of 4th Q, therefore one extra period is needed, bringing the total to forty-one.
3. 6th GS and maths must go against 5th S and 4th P, since nothing else in year 6 can use these periods.
4. 4th L must now go against English in year 6, but there are five English and only three periods of 4th L available — two having been used for 6th X_2. The two remaining English therefore go into 5th T.
5. 6th S_1 and S_2 must now go with 5th T and U.

A schematic diagram for the above conclusions is shown in Figure 9.13. Such a situation is of course rather serious since we have uncovered major problems in a priority area of the school. However, all is not lost! We now must decide on one of two courses of action. Either, defer detailed consideration of the sixth year until a later stage, or amend the sixth form on the basis of our analysis to achieve a satisfactory fit. Of the two, the latter is preferable, since we know that changes must be made in year 6 (we assume that in this case fourth and fifth are more vital). It may well be however that the full horror of the situation will not be revealed until we try timetable construction since we have ignored so far some important pieces of information — part-time staff and the general problem of distribution. In a different case we might perhaps decide on a different plan, but it is only the individual timetabler who can make such a choice.

Let us therefore examine the changes that would have to be made to get a better 'fit'. Obviously our attention should be focused on those parts of year 6 that cannot be fitted at present, namely options

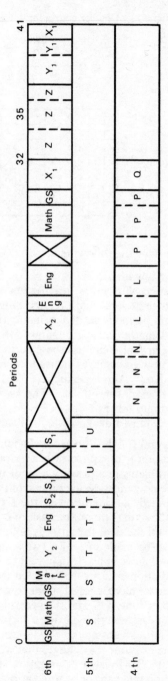

Fig. 9.13 Schematic diagram for 4th, 5th and 6th

Z, Y and X. We want to look first at the positions that are currently unoccupied leaving the established pattern unchanged. If this approach does not produce results, more fundamental changes must of course be considered, but let's try to be as economical as possible.

We could consider initially, for example, the conflicts between 6th Z and 4th N on the grounds that this will both reduce our total requirement by five periods, and also involve looking at conflicts in only one place. We find that, as chance has it, only two teachers prevent a fit (40 and 46). One of these (46) is an art teacher and we know from our previous analysis that art is likely to be problematic because of teams. Consultation with the art department enables 49 to be substituted in year 6. Teacher 40 — a scientist, can similarly be replaced in year 4 by 38 so that we can now place 6th Z against 4th N.

Conveniently enough (and one is sometimes lucky!) we can 'repay' teacher 38 *and* solve another sixth-form clash by changing 38 to 40 in 4th P, enabling 6th Y to fit here and reduce the total periods needed to thirty-five or less.

A further problem is that, since fifth and sixth are together for games, all periods of options in year 5 *must* go against year 6. This is, as it happens, quite easy to correct, but it does entail making a double of general studies in year 6. The revised schematic diagram is shown in Figure 9.14.

We now can turn our attention to the problems of putting together a timetable for years 4 and 5 using the solution space method described in Chapter 8. The analysis already achieved will not of course have been wasted since we have in both the matrix of Figure 9.12 and the schematic diagram of Figure 9.14 useful material which may help us in the next stage.

SOLUTION SPACE ANALYSIS FOR 4th AND 5th YEARS
Following the Law of Parsimony we want to include at this stage only those parts of the 4th and 5th that have major constraints imposed on them. Clearly we must consider the option schemes, but what is not so clear is how much else should be included: several of the staff for English, maths, etc., have constraints. To begin with then, let us consider just the option schemes; we can of course always add to the diagram if we subsequently discover that we have too much freedom and are thus making too many arbitrary decisions.

The basic solution space diagram is shown in Figure 9.15 and the reader should note that it includes all the relevant blockings for part-time staff as given in the notes to Figure 9.1 — e.g. 4th option N cannot go on Wednesday because teacher 44 is involved and is not available then, 4th option Q cannot go on any morning since PE staff are involved and are needed for games throughout the school on each morning.

Fig. 9.14 · Revised schematic diagram for 4th, 5th and 6th

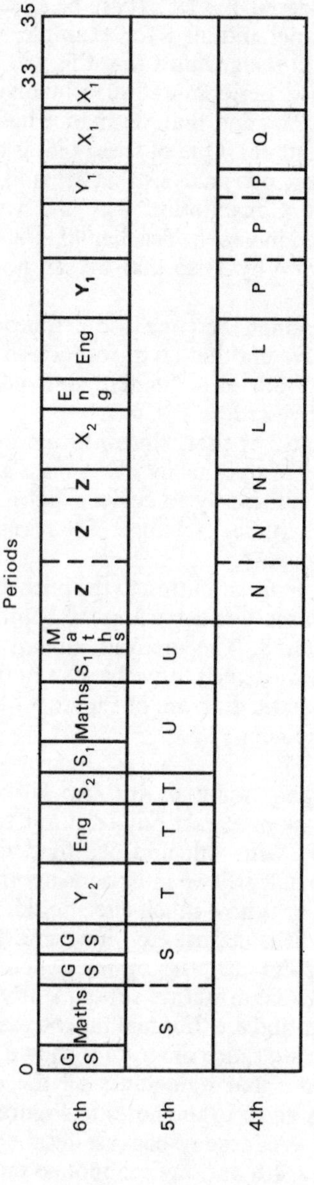

Fig. 9.15 Initial solution space for 4th and 5th options

			MONDAY								TUESDAY								WEDNESDAY								THURSDAY								FRIDAY							
			1	2	3	4	5	6	7	8	1	2	3	4	5	6	7	8	1	2	3	4	5	6	7	8	1	2	3	4	5	6	7	8	1	2	3	4	5	6	7	8
5th	Games	Q	X	X	X	X	X	X	X	X	X	X	X	X	X	X	X	X	X	X	X	X	X	X	X	X	X	X	X	X	X	X	X	X					X	X	X	X
	S	TD								X								X	X	X	X	X	X	X	X	X			X	X				X	X	X	X	X	X	X	X	X
	T	DDS								X								X								X								X	X	X	X	X				X
	U	TD								X								X								X			X	X				X	X	X	X	X				X
4th	Games	Q	X	X	X	X	X	X	X	X	X	X	X	X	X	X	X	X	X	X	X	X	X	X	X	X					X	X	X	X	X	X	X	X	X	X	X	X
	N	DDS								X								X	X	X	X	X	X	X	X	X	X	X	X	X				X								X
	L	TD								X								X	X	X	X	X	X	X	X	X	X	X	X	X				X								X
	P	DDS	X	X	X	X	X	X	X	X	X	X	X	X	X	X	X	X								X	X	X	X	X				X								X
	Q	D	X	X	X	X				X	X	X	X	X				X	X	X	X	X				X	X	X	X	X				X	X	X	X	X				X

Using the general method described in Chapter 8 the steps in the analysis are as follows:

1. 4th option P must use Thursday 5–7 since three days are required. It is probably best to put the single on Thursday since this leaves two periods for English, social studies, etc., whereas a double would leave only one. (The morning is used for games.) Since we know that 4th- and 5th-year options are in conflict throughout (see Figure 9.11 and related text) we can now block Thursday 7 (selected arbitrarily) for all 5th-year options. The remainder of Thursday also becomes blocked for 4th option P.
2. Unless 5th option T goes on Thursday 3 or 4 or both, then we shall create an impossible situation later on. The structure (see Figure 9.11) demands thirty-two unique periods for options and this means that the games *must* be placed against at least one period of options in each year. A single is assumed as the minimum requirement.
3. 4th option P must use Wednesday. If we use the afternoon then we lose a position for a triple period of options of which there are three altogether. We have already lost one triple by using Thursday 7 for 4th P and we know also that 4th Q must use another afternoon. Since Wednesday morning is symmetrical for 4th and 5th (i.e. each period has the same constraints), we choose periods 1 and 2 arbitrarily, blocking these periods for all 5th year options and the remainder of the day for 4th option P.
4. Similarly we put 4th P on Friday 3 and 4, and can then block all remaining periods for this activity since it is complete.

The diagram at this stage is shown in Figure 9.16.

5. We next consider the triple periods together with 4th Q. We know that this set of activities is constrained to afternoons because a triple in a morning would cross break and also would spoil a position for a double period of which we need a lot. For these activities we know the following:

   5th S can use Monday or Tuesday;
   5th U can use Monday, Tuesday, Wednesday or Friday;
   4th L can use Monday, Tuesday or Friday;
   4th Q can use any afternoon.

   We also know by reference to the matrix of Figure 9.12 that 6th option X_2 must go with 4th L, and because 6th X_2 includes teacher 60 (a part-timer) we deduce that we must put 4th L on Monday afternoon. This is a fine example of a part-time teacher (60) imposing his constraint on an option or team in which he is not directly involved.
6. We now are forced to place 5th S on Tuesday afternoon, since Monday, the only other position for the triple, is lost by step 5.

Fig. 9.16 Partly completed solution space analysis

Class	Activity	No.	MONDAY								TUESDAY								WEDNESDAY								THURSDAY								FRIDAY							
			1	2	3	4	5	6	7	8	1	2	3	4	5	6	7	8	1	2	3	4	5	6	7	8	1	2	3	4	5	6	7	8	1	2	3	4	5	6	7	8
5th	Games	Q	X	X	X	X	X	X	X	X	X	X	X	X	X	X	X	X	X	X	X	X	X	X	X	X	X	X	X	X	X	X	X	X					X	X	X	X
	S	TD								X								X	X	X	X	X	X	X	X	X			X	X			X	X	X	X	X	X	X	X	X	X
	T	DDS								X								X	X	X						X	X	X			X	X	X	X	X	X	X	X				X
	U	TD								X								X	X	X						X			X	X			X	X	X	X	X	X				X
4th	Games	Q	X	X	X	X	X	X	X	X	X	X	X	X	X	X	X	X	X	X	X	X	X	X	X	X					X	X	X	X	X	X	X	X	X	X	X	X
	N	DDS								X								X	X	X	X	X	X	X	X	X	X	X	X	X			X	X			X	X				X
	L	TD								X								X	X	X	X	X	X	X	X	X	X	X	X	X			X	X			X	X				X
	P	DDS	X	X	X	X	X	X	X	X	X	X	X	X	X	X	X	X			X	X	X	X	X	X	X	X	X	X	X	X		X	X	X			X	X	X	X
	Q	D	X	X	X	X				X	X	X	X	X				X	X	X	X	X				X	X	X	X	X			X	X	X	X	X	X				X

7. 5th U we now put on Wednesday 5–7 since if we use Friday we have no periods left for English, maths, social studies, etc. Also we notice that none of the 4th-year options can use *all* of Wednesday afternoon.

8. Since we know we must keep Tuesday available for 4th-year English, etc. (see step 1), we now put 4th Q on Friday afternoon. Notice that we now block Friday 5 for 5th U since we have no singles of this activity. Friday 5 for 5th T however, remains free even though we have for the time being placed the single on Thursday — we may later change our minds and make this a double.

   The analysis at this stage is shown in Figure 9.17.

9. At this stage we appear to have a fair amount of freedom and we should therefore consider carefully the possible effect of our alternatives on the feasibility of the sixth form. This can be done by extending our diagram to show the sixth-form activities and their conflicts with the fourth- and fifth-year activities so far entered. Use of the matrix of Figure 9.12 (revised to take account of the changes we have made) makes this quite simple.

   The new diagram is shown in Figure 9.18.

   This diagram also contains some more blockings arising from a consideration of the new information considered. We have for instance determined that 6th option Z shall go with 4th option N and therefore periods where one is blocked become blocked for the other and vice versa. Also we have entered some of the information presented in Figure 9.14: the arrangement of sixth-form activities with the triples of 4th L and 5th S, and with 4th Q. Additional blockings that may at first sight seem unnecessary are for 4th N and L on Friday. In the schematic diagram of Figure 9.14 we have sixth-form activities against all of N and L in year 4. No sixth-form activity can go on Friday morning since the games is there already. Therefore we can have neither N nor L in year 4.

10. Examination of Figure 9.18 shows that we can complete the fourth and fifth options and the entire sixth year in a variety of ways depending on where we decide to start. Figure 9.19 has been selected from several alternatives on the grounds that a better distribution of options results, even though we lose periods 5 and 6 on Thursday for year 4 for English, etc. Here again we are satisfying our requirements in a hierarchical way, the absolute requirements first, followed by desirable requirements. Figure 9.19 shows the completed analysis. It may of course be necessary to revise Figure 9.19 when we come to consider the remainder of years 4 and 5, but if a record of the allocation is kept, this enables a retracing to be easily done.

Fig. 9.17 Solution space analysis nearing completion

Fig. 9.18 Revised diagram including 6th form

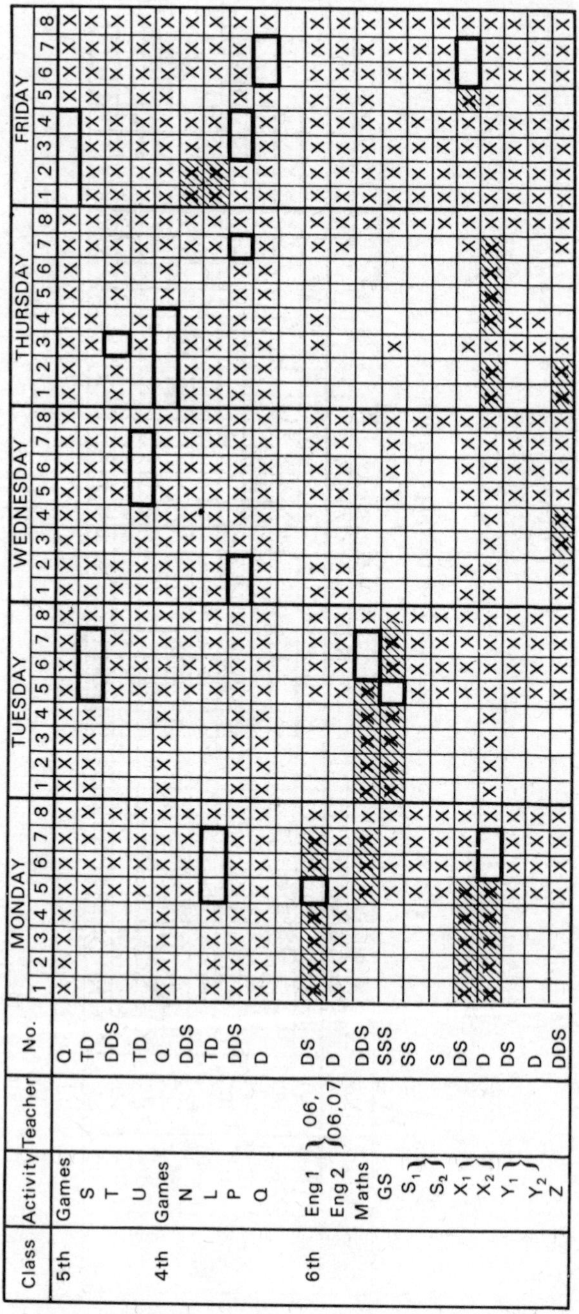

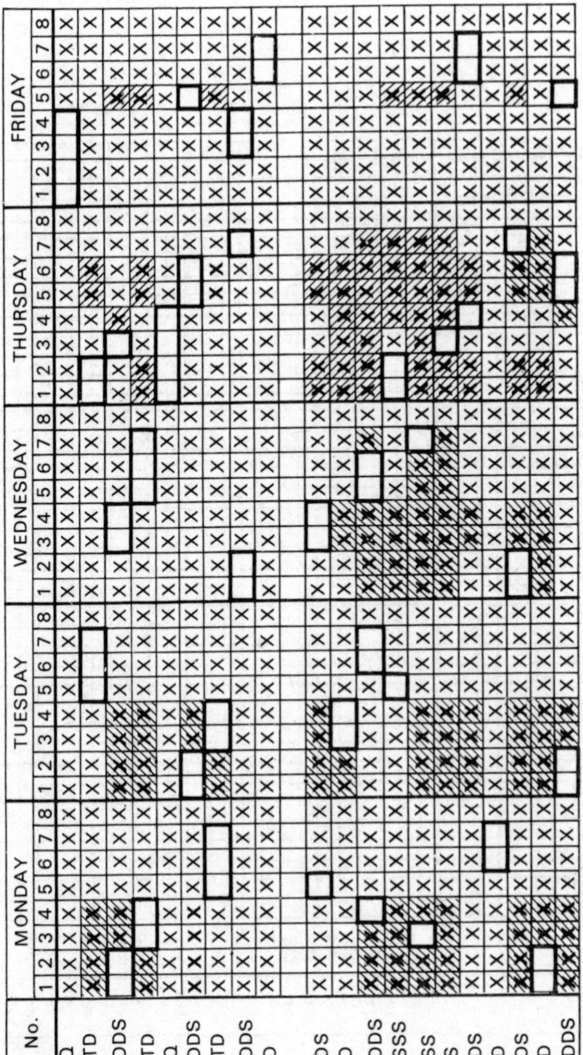

Fig. 9.19 Completed analysis for year 6 and options in 4th and 5th

Fig. 9.20 Schematic solution space for remainder of 5th year

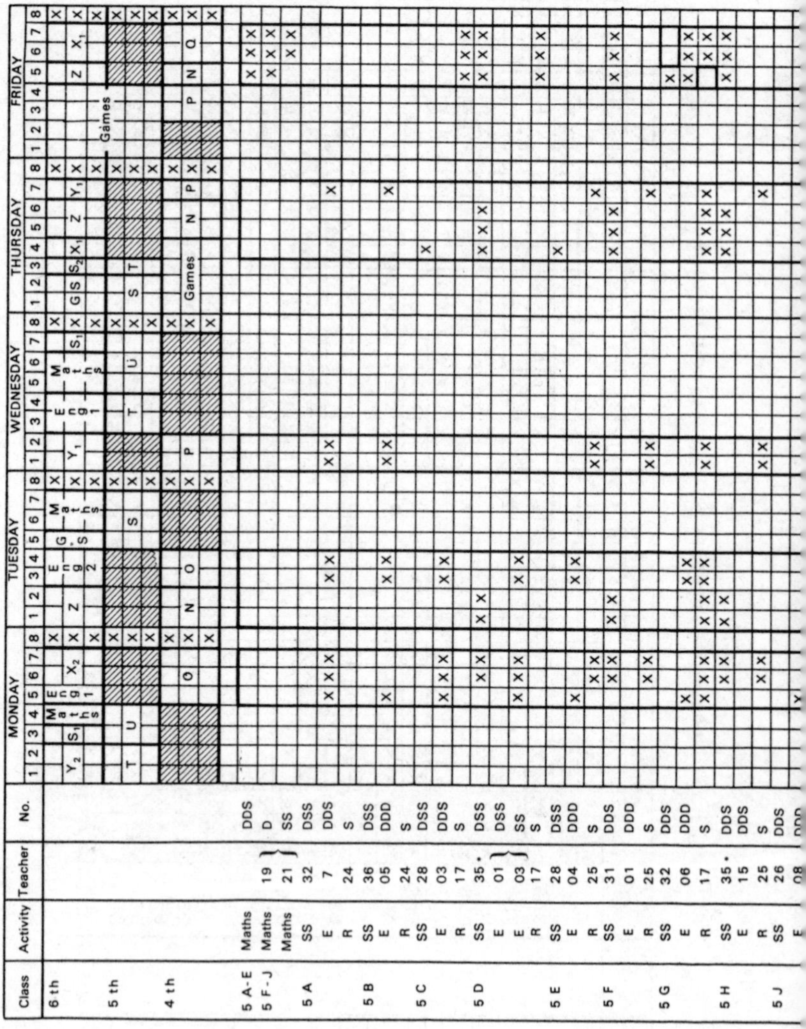

A similar technique can be adopted for the continuation of the analysis. We now know where the options in years 4 and 5 are to go, and also the complete sixth form. This means that we can limit the solution space for the remainder of years 4 and 5 because a proportion of the week for each is already placed and also because of conflicts with activities already placed in other years. The timetable so far, and the limitations imposed in the rest of year 5 are shown in Figure 9.20.

Several features of Figure 9.20 are of interest. First, as stated earlier, we need consider in the fifth year only those periods that are unoccupied by fifth-year options or games — i.e., we can eliminate from consideration all but sixteen periods of the week. Second we have grouped together the subjects for each class (with the exception of maths) since this makes it easier to see the consequences of blocked periods in one subject for the periods of another. And finally we have included the teachers concerned to make reference simpler.

The analysis of such a diagram clearly follows the same general principles as already discussed, but in addition we must bear in mind that the same teacher sometimes appears for more than one class. This may mean — as with teacher 35 (asterisked in Figure 9.20), that although the classes individually may appear to have enough periods available — four for 5D, five for 5H — when taken *together* we find that it is impossible to have both: there are only six available periods for both 5D and 5H.

Figure 9.20 also shows up the fact that 5G (social studies) is the only activity for this class that can use Friday 6 and 7, and 5G is thus forced to this position, thus itself forcing RE to period 5. These allocations clearly block the relevant teachers and classes in these periods as shown.

CONCLUSION

This analysis could clearly be continued: we have not for example resolved the problems with art and craft, nor have we completed the timetable for years 4 and 5. In my opening remarks in Chapter 1 I made the point that I doubted if this book offered a complete answer to the problems of planning and construction. Having now reached the end I am more convinced than before of this! At the same time I am heartened by the ground that has been covered: it is in all honesty rather more than I had expected! It is my hope that the timetablers who read this book will have found it useful and stimulating, and that they will put into practice at least some of the techniques.

10   A do-it-yourself example

In this final chapter the reader is given an opportunity to try for himself some of the methods and techniques described in the book. The example has deliberately been kept straightforward in the hope that results will be obtained easily, giving encouragement for further practical applications.

In Figure 10.1 the basic curriculum is given together with certain other information. The text that follows should enable the reader to check his progress.

Notes – the headmaster (needed later on!) can only teach on Wednesday 4 and 5
  – Teacher 31 only teaches on Mon. 1–5, Tue. 1–5, Wed. (all day)
  – Teachers 27 and 29 only teach on Tues. 1–5. Wed. 1–5. Thurs. 1–5. Fri. (all day)
  – 5th Games (Ga) must be Thurs. 6–8
  – 4th Games   must be Tues. 6–8
  – 3rd Games   must be Mon. 6–8
  – There are 5 days in the week, each with 8 periods. Break after period 3 Lunch after period 5

1. You should start with the analysis of the science department and thereafter follow the instructions as relevant to your progress.
2. *Analysis of science department*
   2.1. Is the staffing of science, including options in years 4 and 5 in which science appears, feasible?
   2.2. If your analysis shows that the science requirements are impossible to meet, go to step 5. Otherwise go to step 3.
3. You should check your analysis of science teams. If you still cannot demonstrate infeasibility, go to step 4 and check with the answer given.
4. Your analysis of science teams should be along the following lines:
   4.1. Select the critical resource. That some science staff appear in games can be ignored.
   4.2. Insert *all* periods for critical resource (04), as on Figure 10.2.
   4.3. Select the resource with the largest number of periods remaining. This is the new critical resource. Either 01 or 02 will do.

Fig. 10.1 The curriculum

Year 5

	Opt 1 DDS	Opt 2 DDS	Opt 3 TD	Opt 4 TD	Opt 5 DDS	Maths SSSSS	Ga T	Eng SSSSS	R S	C S
5A	01	02	23	25	01	15	21	07	13	14
B	02	04	24	26	06	16	22	08	13	14
C	05	05	28	29	13	17	01	09	13	14
D	32	33	36	30	36	18	13	10	13	14
E	35	34	38	35	39	19	14	11	13	14
F	37	41		40	40	20	42	11	13	14
					14					

Year 4

	TD	TD	DDS	DDS	Opt 5 DDS	Maths SSSSS	Ga T	Eng SSSSS	S	S
4A	23	26	01	02	02	15	21	07	13	14
B	24	27	04	04	03	16	22	08	13	14
C	25	28	30	06	06	17	18	09	13	14
D	31	42	34	13	35	18	30	10	13	14
E	36	14	36	38	33	19	34	12	13	14
F				40	36	20	42	12	13	14

Year 3

	Hum. DDD	Craft TT	Ga T	Science DDD	French SSSS	Maths SSSSS	Eng. SSSSS	PE D	μ SS	R S
3A	36	23	21	01,02,03,04	32	15	07	21	30	13
B	37	24	22		33	16	08	22	30	13
C	38	25	01		34	17	11	21	30	13
D	39	26	14	03,04,05,06	32	18	08	22	31	13
E	40	27	18		34	19	09	21	31	13
F	41	28			35	20	12	22	31	13
	42	29								

Key R = RE   Science staff
     C = Careers   01–06
     Ga = Games
     μ = Music

Fig. 10.2

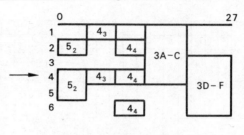

Fig. 10.3

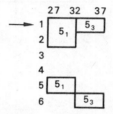

4.4. Insert periods for new critical resource that:
     (a) are in conflict with all periods so far inserted;
     (b) are forced to certain positions. See Figure 10.3.
4.5. Complete the analysis by inserting the remaining team,
     bringing the total periods to forty-two. The science teams
     are thus infeasible. (Many are tempted to place two fifth-
     year options in the *same* periods, but this is of course in-
     correct!)
4.6. Go to step 5.
5. The head of science suggests altering one of the third-year teams
   so that it will fit with either 4_3 or 5_5. Is this sufficient? (Hint:
   check the number of double periods.)
   5.1. If your analysis suggests that changing one third-year team
        is sufficient, go to step 6. If you think more changes are
        needed, go to step 7.
6. Changing one third-year team does of course enable the science
   to occupy less than forty periods. However, it is not sufficient
   when you take into consideration the number of double periods
   required. In the initial requirements we have eighteen double
   periods. The structure of the day is such that only three doubles
   can occur, giving a maximum of fifteen in the week.

$$
\begin{array}{c}
\text{periods} \\
\begin{array}{c|cc|ccc}
1\ 2\ 3 & 4\ 5 & 6\ 7\ 8
\end{array}
\end{array}
$$

$$5 \times \quad \boxed{D1} \quad \boxed{D2} \quad \boxed{D3} \quad = \quad 15\ \text{doubles}$$

Changing one third-year team reduces the number of doubles to sixteen since two of the third-year doubles will be simultaneous with science in year 4 or 5. Sixteen doubles is still too many. Now go to step 7.

7. Yes. It is necessary to change *both* third-year teams to reduce the number of unique doubles to below the maximum of fifteen. The head of science accepts this necessity and suggests new third-year teams as follows:

   3A–C   02, 03, 04, 05
   3D–F   02, 03, 05, 06

   7.1 Amend the curriculum to take account of these changes.
   7.2. Go to either step 8 or step 13.

8. *Analysis of 3rd-year structure*
   8.1. Using a schematic diagram, make an analysis of the third-year curriculum. Is the curriculum structurally sound?
   8.2. If your answer to 8.1. is 'Yes' go to step 9 and follow the analysis given. If 'No' go to step 10.

9. The problematic part of the third year is the PE, RE, music area. The double PE for 3A and B, and for 3E and F must be simultaneous with RE and Music for 3C and 3D respectively since there is no other subject of the correct 'shape'. For 3C and D PE however, it is impossible — given the staffing constraints — to occupy all other classes for the relevant periods. A similar problem arises for the second period of music.
   Figure 10.4 shows many periods — marked X — that cannot be used. The shaded area can be used by any subject taught to half-year groups. Now go to step 10.

10. The headmaster agrees to take two third-year classes for RE and the music department agrees that staff can be re-allocated. Do these suggestions solve the problem? If you think the problem is resolved, go to step 11. If not, go to step 12.

11. These suggestions do of course improve matters, but there are still problems as shown in the revised diagram. Figure 10.5. Now continue with step 12.

Fig. 10.4

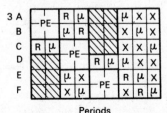

Periods

Fig. 10.5

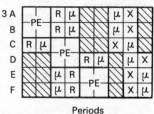

Periods

12. Right. We still have problems! With great reluctance the music department agrees to 'borrow' teacher 20 (maths) who plays trombone in the local brass band. This enables three classes to have music simultaneously, as shown in Figure 10.6 (with the headmaster taking 3B and 3F for RE).

Fig. 10.6

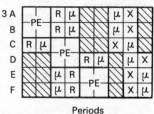

Periods

12.1. Amend curriculum to take account of these changes.
12.2. Have you analysed the option schemes in the fourth and fifth? If yes, go to 27, if no go to step 13.

13. *Analysis of fourth and fifth years*
The central issue here is whether the options in years 4 and 5 will 'fit'. This should be approached in two stages:
13.1 What set of conditions must be satisfied if options are to fit?
13.2. Are these conditions fulfilled? (Use a conflict matrix.)
If you are unsure of 13.1, go to 14 for an explanation.
If your answer to 13.2 is 'Yes' go to 15. If 'No' go to 16.

14. Since there are twenty-five periods of options in each year, there must be an overlap of at least ten periods, as shown in Figure 10.7.
Now go back to 13.2.

15. There are exactly ten periods overlap. The matrix required is shown in Figure 10.8.
Options 1 and 2 must clearly go together and moreover the triple periods in year 4 must be set against the singles in year 5.

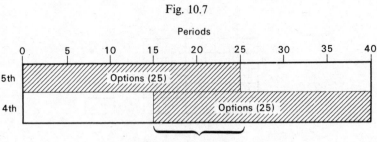

Fig. 10.7

Fig. 10.8

15.1. Having established that a fit is possible, what else can you discover about the fourth and fifth? For example, what about double and triple periods?

15.2. If you can find no difficulty with multiple periods in the option scheme, go to step 16. If you have discovered any infeasibility, go to step 18.

16. Check your analysis carefully, I think you have an error! Compare your matrix with that given in Figure 10.8.

17. Even though neither fourth nor fifth taken alone presents any apparent problem with respect to multiple periods, we must consider what happens when the two years are combined. We know from step 14 that there must be ten periods overlap and from step 15 that the overlap will be between options 1 and 2 in each year. This overlap will give us two triples and two doubles. (See Figure 10.9). In addition the remaining thirty periods (fifteen in each year) include two triples and ten doubles. The total requirement is thus for four triples and twelve doubles as

Fig. 10.9

5	1	2		2	1			1	2		2	1
4	1			2			or	1			2	

Fig. 10.10

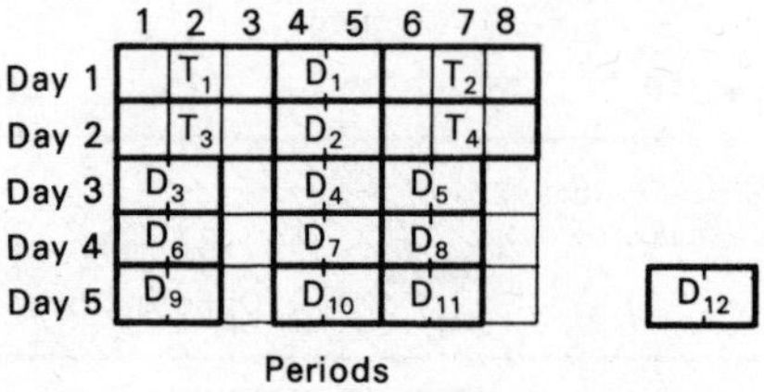

Periods

shown in Figure 10.10. This is not possible within the structure of the week.

Now continue with 18.

18. Very reluctantly the head of science agrees to change 4th option 3 from two doubles and one single to one double and three singles. The head of languages is delighted by this!

    18.1. Does this solve the problem?

    18.2. If your answer is 'Yes' go to step 20. If 'No' go to step 19.

19. Splitting a double in 4th option 3 reduces the number of doubles to eleven and this is just possible. Check your analysis and then continue to 20.

20. Correct. All is now O.K. with doubles and triples. Can you find any other problems with the fourth- or fifth-year structure? (Try a schematic diagram.) If you can find nothing structurally wrong, go to step 21, otherwise go to 22.

21. The problem with fourth (or fifth) is similar to the third-year problem (step 9), but here it is English that causes difficulty. In year 5 we have all classes together for 25 periods of options + 3 games + 5 maths = 33 periods. This means that the English, RE and careers are forced to the same seven periods for all classes. Since English is five periods, we cannot have the same teacher for two classes as stated. Exactly the same situation occurs in year 4.

Now continue with 22.

22. The head of English agrees to swap teachers 11 and 12 in 5F and 4E respectively. Both teams now read 07, 08, 09, 10, 11, 12.

    22.1. Amend curriculum to take account of these changes.

    22.2. All other things being equal, what can you say about the distribution of English in fourth and fifth? Will every class have English on each day of the week?

    22.3. If you answer 'Yes' to 22.2 go to 23. If 'No' go to 24.

23. Each of the seven periods available for English, RE, careers must contain at least four classes of English, and English must appear for some set of classes in all seven periods. Many arrangements are possible, but none allows every class to have English once on each of five days. See, for example, Figure 10.11. If 5A, B, C, and D use five days for English as shown, then 5E

Fig. 10.11

Day no.

		1	2	1	2	3	4	5 Day
5	A	R	C	E	E	E	E	E
	B	C	R	E	E	E	E	E
Class	C	E	E	R	C	E	E	E
	D	E	E	C	R	E	E	E
	E	E	E	E	E	R	C	E
	F	E	E	E	E	C	R	E

Periods

and 5F have two days on which there must be two periods of English.

Continue with 24.

24. Good. Some classes must have two periods of English on some days. Impressed by the inevitability of your argument the head of English simply asks you to do your best.

What else can you deduce about the fourth- and fifth-year structure? If you think all is now well, go to 25. If not, go to 26.

25. There are still problems! We know from the matrix (Figure 10.8) that options 3, 4 and 5 in both years are in complete conflict. We therefore know that games, English and maths must go with these options. Using matrices this deduction can be tested. You should therefore construct two additional matrices as shown in 26.

26. Games, maths and English in years 4 and 5 must go with options 3, 4, and 5. The conflicts are shown in the two matrices in Figure 10.12.

Note 'E' here includes RE and careers. Since the seven periods are almost identical in their resource requirements we can justify the simplification of treating all periods as identical. However these matrices are analysed — and there are a number of alternatives — we can never achieve a complete fit, unless we

Fig. 10.12

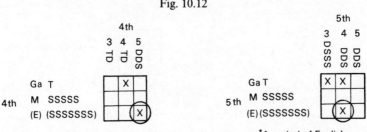

*1 period of English
(without 13 or 14)
can go in those
positions marked (X)

Fig. 10.13

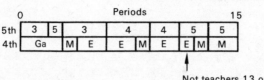

are prepared to accept changing either the resources or the period breakdown or both.

In the matrix of 5th 3, 4, 5 v 4th Ga, M, E we must place a single of 5_5 against 4th Ga to avoid having two doubles of maths in year 4. From this starting point a pattern emerges as shown in Figure 10.13, with a consequent double of maths and doubling of English. This latter is not too serious since a double English will not be a double of the subject in all classes since RE and careers are intermingled.

In the matrix of 4th 3, 4, 5 v 5th Ga, M, E we must change resources to avoid doubling 5th maths twice against 4_4. This can be done by removing teacher 13 from 5th games. This also resolves the problem of being unable to cover 5th games completely since we can now use both options 4 and 5. The revised matrix is shown in Figure 10.14.

Exploration of this matrix shows that unless 4_4 (D) goes with 5th games we must double maths. Also that to avoid doubling maths at all we must put one period of English (without teacher 13) against the remaining double of 4_4. The pattern in Figure 10.15 therefore can be established.

26.1. Continue with step 8 if you have *not* looked at year 3; otherwise go on to 27.

Fig. 10.14

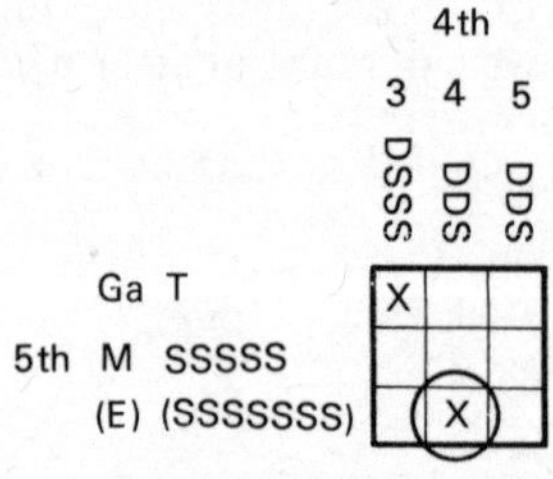

Fig. 10.15

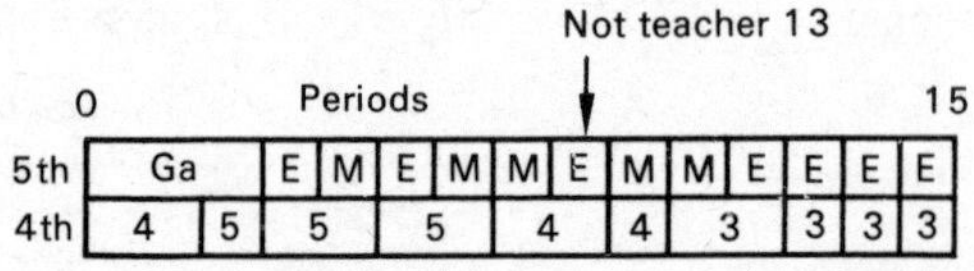

27. We have now established a pattern for years 4 and 5. We can next consider the implications of this pattern for year 3. A schematic matrix is probably the easiest way of doing so, but one could first attempt a timetable for years 4 and 5 using a solution space diagram. A schematic matrix is shown in Figure 10.16. From this matrix it is clear that further changes will be necessary. For example, humanities cannot be placed anywhere because none of the fourth or fifth have conflict-free positions that can be used. Note also that third games, and the final pattern for options 1 and 2 have still to be fixed.

    What changes would you recommend in order to place humanities and games? Do you need to make any other changes? Go on to step 28.

28. Many solutions are possible of course and in practical cases one will often be able to determine a 'Best' solution from educational considerations. In this exercise we do not have the benefit of such educational decisions and so must choose those alternatives that affect fewest resources.

    In the humanities we can either drop teacher 36 or 40, but 36 is preferable since we then have the required three doubles. The games is rather harder but $14 \rightarrow 42$ and $18 \rightarrow 34$ enables games to go with 5th 3 and 4th M, E, all of which can go on Monday 6–8. To complete the pattern for the third year further changes are required. The exact changes will depend again on local circumstances, but one solution, given here, necessitates further changes to science and also to French. The following shows the order of working to give a complete pattern, and also shows the changes needed:

    1. Hu v 4_5, 4_3 (teacher 36 removed from 3rds).
    2. Ga v 5_3 (T) (teacher $18 \rightarrow 34$, $14 \rightarrow 42$ in games).
    3. R/PE/μ, μ/PE/R v 4_4, 5M, 5E double.[1]
    4. C v 5_5, 5E twice to give triples na.
    5. Placing of Ga (2) and C (4) makes science impossible. By reducing teams we can however get complete setting with the entire science department.

    $$S \text{ v } 5_3, 5_4 \text{ (DDD) na.}$$

    (An alternative would of course be to give science a higher priority, thus having to change both craft and games.)

---

[1] an alternative is:
   3. 3A — C F 3D — F F v 4_4, 5E, M double.
This makes little difference except that only one period of French in each third-year group needs changing instead of two. The remaining steps are of course slightly different.

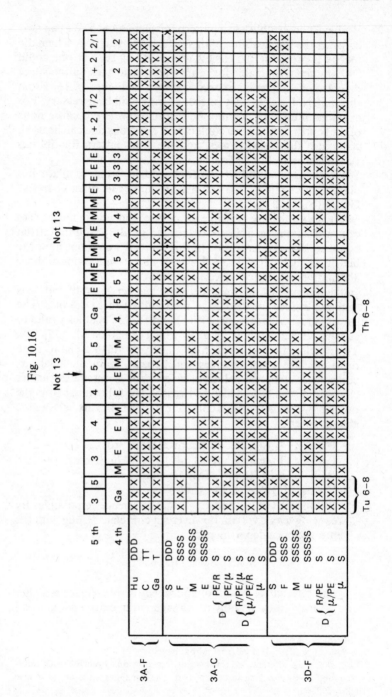

Fig. 10.16

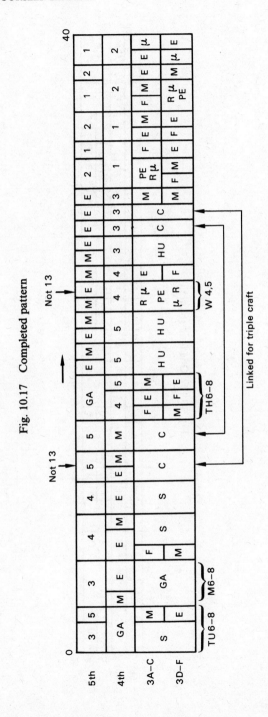

Fig. 10.17 Completed pattern

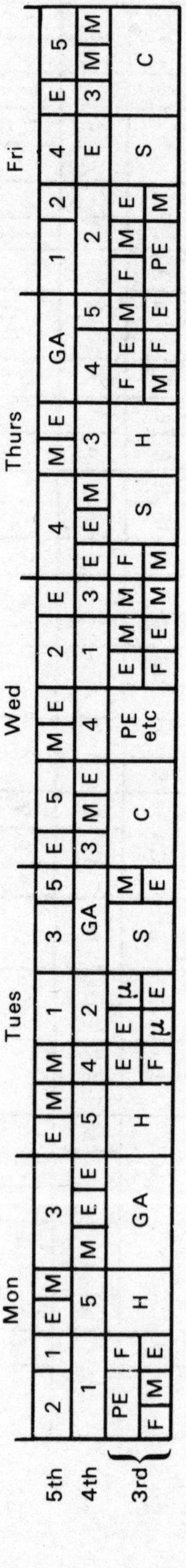

Fig. 10.18 One final solution

6. 3D — FE v 4Ga na.
7. ∴ 3A — CM v 4Ga na.
8. μ v 4_2 double.
9. F, M, E v 5th Games na.
10. $3A - C$ F/E, $3D - F$ E/F v 5_M 4_4 single. Choose $3D - F$ F, $3A - C$ E (an arbitrary selection).
11. Remaining periods of French (two in each half-year) are impossible. By changing teams either for all periods or for remaining two only we can accommodate French under 4_1 4_2 in $3A–C$ $32 \rightarrow 41$ (goes with 5_1). In $3D–F$ $34 \rightarrow 38$ (goes with 5_2).
12. PE/R, PE/μ, etc. Placed against triples to reduce chances of doubling in E, M, F.
13. Remaining periods of E, M, F to give pattern as shown in 10.17.

The final stage is to take account of distribution of this pattern to the days of the week using a solution space diagram. This will show that distribution of all subjects cannot be perfect with the particular part-time requirements, so it will be a matter of deciding which is more essential. If we go for good distribution then we must accept changes to part-timers, and vice versa. In this case assume that part-time requirements are more important. One possible solution is shown in Figure 10.18.

Index